# I AM NOT MY THOUGHTS

Be Your Own Boss Over Your Thoughts!
Overcome Barriers, Challenges, and Regrets!!!

**Harrison S. Mungal, Ph.D, Psy.D**

# I Am Not My Thoughts

Copyright © 2024 Harrison S. Mungal

All rights reserved. Neither this publication nor any part of this publication may be reproduced or transmitted in any form or by any means, electronic or mechanical, including photocopying, recording or any information storage and retrieval system, without permission in writing from the author.

Contact author via email: info@harrisonmungal.com
info@agetoage.ca
www.agetoage.ca
www.harrisonmungal.com
www.harrisonmungalbooks.com
Facebook: Harrison Mungal
Twitter: AgeToAgeInc1
LinkedIn: Harrison Mungal, Ph.D., PsyD
YouTube: Harrison Mungal
Phone: 905-533-1334

# About The Author

With an extensive background in clinical psychology, Harrison is deeply committed to enhancing the lives of those he counsels. His academic credentials are impressive, boasting dual doctoral degrees in Clinical Psychology and Philosophy in Social Work and two master's degrees in Social Work and Counselling. He also holds a Bachelor's degree in Theology. His areas of expertise encompass mental health, addiction, marital and relationship, family dynamics, and parenting issues.

Recognized as a leading authority in cognitive therapy, Harrison is a sought-after presenter at workshops. His multifaceted role allows him to assist individuals, couples, families, and corporations. Harrison, a global public speaker, has addressed audiences in over 42 countries at various conferences, seminars, and public events. His reach extends to radio and television appearances, and he has authored over 40 books (including translation in Spanish, German, French and others to be determine). He is widely respected for his profound insights, as well as his engaging sense of humour and enthusiasm for subjects like mental health, addictions, relationships, and parenting.

Harrison's approach to his work is both inventive and grounded in scientific principles. This unique methodology has earned him a sterling reputation, along with multiple awards and accolades from an array of institutions, including law enforcement agencies, municipal governments, community leaders, and corporate executives. He offers training and consultations to a diverse range of community partners, including medical professionals, social workers, first responders, law enforcement officials, and senior management teams.

An active participant in cognitive research, Harrison has led several ground-breaking studies aimed at aiding people with mental health issues like addiction, psychosis, anxiety, and depression. Among these studies are explorations into music therapy for schizophrenia, vaccination protocols for young children, and the role of substance abuse in the food service industry. His work on Thought Developmental Practice (TDP) has been particularly notable for providing alternative treatments for conditions like substance abuse, anxiety, PTSD, and depression.

With over two decades of professional experience, Harrison has worked with a broad and diverse range of populations. His experience encompasses over 21 years in the mental health and psychiatry fields and more than a decade as a practicing clinical psychotherapist. He has provided services to a myriad of communities, including those affected by Acquired Brain Injuries, refugees, victims of warfare, and individuals in crisis across various settings, which include collaborations with police forces, hospitals, community agencies, and inpatient mental health facilities.

In terms of therapeutic approaches, Harrison is well-versed in a wide array of evidence-based treatments. These include, but are not limited to, Cognitive Behavioural Therapy (CBT), Cognitive Processing Therapy (CPT), Dialectical Behavioural Therapy (DBT), and Acceptance and Commitment Therapy (ACT). He is also skilled in Interpersonal Therapy (IPT), Motivational Interviewing Techniques, Grounding Techniques, and various other specialized forms of treatment, such as Humanistic Experiential Therapy and Psychodynamic Therapy.

Author: Harrison S. Mungal, BTh, MCC, MSW, PhD, PsyD.

# Introduction

From the time we are born, many things shape the way we think. Our culture, family, schooling, parenting, marriage, and jobs all play a part in building our thoughts and how we see ourselves and the world. If we grow up in a family that values hard work or education, a push to work hard, it adds to the complexity of our thoughts. Same would apply to those who were raised in a dysfunctional home, where addictions, abuse, trauma and even being raised by a single parent affects our thinking. It's important to remember that thoughts themselves aren't good or bad, it's what we do with them that really matters.

As children, our minds are like sponges soaking up everything around us. This shapes the views and biases that might stay with us our whole lives. But our thinking doesn't have to stay the same. Over time, we can change the way we think. This ability to change our thoughts can make a big difference. It can help us move past harmful thinking patterns and become more flexible in our thinking.

Our dreams and goals often mix imagination with real life. As children, we're told to dream big. These dreams can give us hope and motivation. However, it's important to know the difference between what we wish for and what we can actually do. If we don't, we might try to escape reality in harmful ways, leading to making wrong decision, bad choices, and regrets that can weigh us down.

We often focus more on negative thoughts than positive ones. This might come from feeling insecure, not confident, or from situations that point out our flaws. Instead of blaming ourselves or others, we should try to understand why we think this way. We need to learn how to separate ourselves and others from problems and target the problem and not the person.

Our beliefs also play a big role in how we think. Being open to new ideas and ready to question our own beliefs can help us grow mentally. If we stick too firmly to old beliefs, we limit how much we can learn and grow.

There are different parts of our brain are responsible for different kinds of thinking. Some of us might be more logical and analytical, while others are more creative and emotional. Whether or not we have a clear plan for our lives can either make our thoughts more chaotic or give us a sense of direction.

Thoughts are also influenced by the world around us. Advice from someone we respect or a mean comment from someone else can change how we feel and think. Our perceptions can have a negative impact on our lives more than we can imagine. Being bullied or manipulated can mess with our ability to think clearly and make us doubt ourselves.

In short, our thoughts are shaped by a mix of our background, culture, beliefs, traditions what we've learned, and our experiences. Even though our thoughts can be complex and influenced by many things, we have the power to change them. By understanding where our thoughts come from and being open to changing them, we can grow mentally and emotionally.

This understanding helps us navigate through our thoughts more effectively, allowing us to change, refine, and even completely transform how we think. Knowing where our thoughts come from not only offers insight into our own minds but also empowers us to guide our thoughts in new, more positive directions.

Unwanted, intrusive thoughts can interrupt our peace of mind. These thoughts usually come from past bad experiences, traumas, or deep fears. Learning how to handle these unwanted thoughts can really help improve our mental health and happiness.

Just like an athlete works hard to be in top shape, we can train our minds to focus on success and well-being. This strong mindset includes being resilient, staying focused, changing our behaviours, choices and always trying to better ourselves.

It's also important to know the difference between what we think and how we feel. Thoughts are usually about figuring things out and are more organized. Feelings are more about sudden reactions and can make it hard to think clearly. Making decisions should not just be about how we feel at the moment, but thinking of the bigger picture, the future. Thinking things through always lead to better decisions.

The things we do every day, our habits and routines, shapes how we feel and what we think. Healthy habits and positivity think will produce less regrets.

Seeing yourself as the main character in your life means accepting both your strengths and weakness, you flaw and imperfections. We need to strengthen our strengths and build our weaknesses to avoid negative thoughts and unwanted feelings.

Finally, seeing ourselves as others see us can give us a complete picture of who we are and how we think. This means being honest with ourselves, recognizing our faults, and pursuing to become better than our best. By doing this, we can overcome obstacles, take on challenges, and move past regrets. This leads to a life that's more rewarding and meaningful. This book will help your understand you thoughts and how to get rid of unwanted intrusive thoughts that is affecting you day-today life. Your will be empowered to tap into the power of resiliency to become an achiever in life.

# Table Of Content

Introduction .................................................................................. 5
Chapter 1 The Origins Of Thought ...................................... 15
Chapter 2 The Intricacies Of Thought Processes ............... 21
    Thoughts Shape Reality .................................................... 23
    No "Right" Or "Wrong": The Relativity Of Thought ..... 25
Chapter 3 Fantasy And Reality Thinking ............................ 27
    The Genesis Of Fantasy: Dreams, Visions, And Goals .... 27
    The Risks And Causes Of Escapism ................................ 29
    Reality Thinking: The Grounding Force ......................... 31
Chapter 4 Why Do I Think More Negative Thoughts Than Positive Ones? ........................................................................ 35
    Insecurities ........................................................................ 35
    Lack Of Confidence ......................................................... 38
    Low Self-Esteem .............................................................. 39
    Pride And Ego .................................................................. 41
Chapter 5 Thoughts Are Affected By Beliefs - The Intrinsic Web Of Mindset ........................................................................ 45

Beliefs In Personal Superiority ................................................................. 45

Lack Of A Student Mind ............................................................................. 46

Allowing Personality And Character To Rule ....................................... 48

Resistance To Change ................................................................................. 48

Stuck In One's Generation ......................................................................... 50

Information Processing .............................................................................. 51

## Chapter 6 Left Brain And Right Brain Thinker .................................. 53

Impact On Relationships ........................................................................... 54

Strengths And Weaknesses Of The Left-Brain Thinker And Right-Brain Thinker ................................................................................................ 55

Introversion And Extroversion ................................................................ 58

## Chapter 7 Lack Of A Blueprint .................................................................. 61

How Blueprints Are Formed .................................................................... 61

Observing Others And Borrowing Ideas .............................................. 62

Piggybacking On Others ............................................................................ 63

## Chapter 8 Influences ..................................................................................... 67

What Are Influences? ................................................................................. 67

Where Do Influences Come From? ........................................................ 68

How Are We Affected By Influences? ................................................... 69

Positive And Negative Influence Affects Our Thinking ................. 70

What People Say Can Influence Our Thinking .................................. 71

Brain Manipulation: The Dark Side Of Influence ............................. 72

Emotional Bullying As A Form Of Negative Influence ................... 73

## Chapter 9 -Intrusive Thoughts - The Uninvited Mental Guests ........ 75

Where Do Intrusive Thoughts Come From? ....................................... 76

Regrets, Mistakes, And Wrong Choices ................................................ 77

Bad Upbringing ................................................................. 78

Traumas And Abuse ......................................................... 80

Innocence And Blaming Self............................................ 80

Dealing With Passive Thoughts, Planned Thoughts, And Active Thoughts............................................................................ 81

Negative Memory Cards Need To Be Replaced With Positive Ones .................................................................................................. 83

Cancel The Past ................................................................ 84

## Chapter 10 The Intricacies Of Positive And Negative Thought Patterns ................................................................................ 87

How Does The Brain Produce These Thoughts?............. 87

The Neurological Reasoning ............................................ 88

Why Does The Brain Produce Thoughts To Protect Itself?......... 89

The Balancing Act Of Positive And Negative Thoughts ............... 90

## Chapter 11 The Blueprint For Thought Mastery ..................... 93

Who Is A Champion? Think Like An Athlete. .................. 93

Comparing A Champion With Championing Our Thoughts........ 94

The Purpose Of Championing Our Thoughts................. 95

Characteristics And Traits Of A Champion And Their Thoughts 96

Train Your Thoughts Like A Champion........................... 99

## Chapter 12 I Am Not My Thoughts ........................................ 101

Everyone Has Negative And Positive Thoughts ........... 101

Mental Health And Its Relation To Negative Thoughts .............. 102

Stress And Its Relation To Negative Thoughts ............. 103

I Am Not To Blame For My Negative Thoughts........... 105

I Cannot Blame Others For My Negative Thoughts ..... 106

Chapter 13 Break Self-Destructive Thoughts ...................................109
   What Carry Self-Destructive Thoughts.........................................109
      Avoid Feeling Sorry For Yourself..............................................111
      Avoid Narcissistic Personality Traits........................................111
      Avoid Borderline Personality Behaviours................................112
      Avoid Attention-Seeking...........................................................113
      Our Choices Affect Our Thinking ...........................................113
      The Power Of Apologies And Forgiveness..............................115

Chapter 14 Thoughts And Not Feelings ..........................................117
   What's The Difference Between A Thought And A Feeling? .....117
   Control Overthinking - Reduce Worrying....................................118
   Impulsive Thoughts Vs. Processed Thoughts (Think Before You Speak)..................................................................................................119
   Your Thoughts Don't Have To Be Your Feelings ........................119
   Avoid Making Your Feelings Other People's Issues.....................120
   Don't Live By Feelings ....................................................................121
   Feelings As Indicators Of Insecurities............................................122

Chapter 15 Changing Your Habits And Behaviours..........................123
   What Are Negative Habits And Behaviours? ...............................123
   We Become What We Think We Are And What We Do ............124
   Regrets Affect Our Thinking From How We Behave And What We Do .................................................................................................124
   Being Kind Will Change Your Mindset........................................126
   A Heart Of Gratitude Will Help See The Light At The End Of The Tunnel ..................................................................................................126
   Change Negative Behaviours..........................................................127

    Break Bad Habits .................................................................................... 128

Chapter 16 Be Your Own Hero ............................................................. 131

    How To Become A Hero In My Thinking ...................................... 131

    Strengths Of A Hero ........................................................................ 132

    Weaknesses Of A Hero .................................................................... 133

    Strengths And Weaknesses Of My Thoughts ................................ 133

    Turn Obstacles Into Opportunities ................................................ 135

Chapter 17 Be Optimistic - Excel In Positive Thinking ................... 139

    Understand Self-Worth And Self-Value ........................................ 139

    What's The Neurological Basis For Having A Positive Mind And Being Optimistic? ............................................................................. 140

    The Results And Rewards Of Being Positive And Optimistic .... 140

Chapter 18 See Yourself How Others See You ................................. 143

    Do A Self-Assessment And Admit Your Flaws, Weaknesses, Mistakes, Bad Habits, And Incompetence ........................................ 143

    Work On Changing Yourself To Become Better ......................... 144

    Explore The Seeds Of Greatness In You ....................................... 144

    Leave A Good Taste In Others ....................................................... 146

    Help Others To Become Better Than Yourself ............................ 148

    Live By The Golden Rule ................................................................ 148

Conclusion ................................................................................................. 153

Chapter 1

# The Origins of Thought

Our thoughts matter greatly in life. They guide our choices, decisions, and future plans, occurring quietly in our minds. Each person's thoughts are unique, but they do not just randomly start. They begin at home, where we first learn and mature. Parents contribute much here in terms of what they say, how they parent and influence our lives with positive words. Whether they mean to or not, they teach us how to think and see the world. Family traditions and beliefs also sway us in our development of thoughts and what we think about ourselves and others. They are like lenses that colour how we view everything around us. These early home lessons are very important. They teach us how to handle daily tasks, interact with others, and understand our emotions and feelings.

When we start school, our thinking changes as school gives us other perfects in life to consider. School is a new and bigger world compared to our homes, and influence how we see the world. We study many subjects, each one challenging and growing our minds in different ways. Math makes us better at logical thinking and solving problems. Science sparks our curiosity and teaches us the scientific method. Humanities make us think critically, and gym class teaches us about teamwork and discipline.

However, school is not just about what is in the books. It is also about the people and the social life we develop. We learn about boundaries and limitations, what we can and cannot do, what makes us feel good and what affects un negatively. We meet students from different backgrounds and get involved in various activities. These experiences teach us much more than any textbook can and what we can learn from our parents. We learn to communicate, negotiate, and understand others' emotions. Our interactions with teachers and classmates improve our social skills. They teach us about empathy, respect for authority, and how to work in groups.

Grades, exams, and competitions are also a big part of school life. They can be stressful, but they teach us important lessons. They show us how to handle pressure, deal with failures, and celebrate successes. They make us stronger thinkers, ready to face the challenges of the outside world. We learn about realities, the nature of how people function, the cruelty and selfishness of others that are sheltered from our parents. We learn about good and not so good habits, behaviours and self-centeredness. We learn about religion, sex and sexuality, drugs, alcohol, music, art and other important factors that will shape our future. We develop our thinking as we experience what makes us feel good. We learn about addictions and desires that also shape our thoughts. School shapes us into diverse and well-rounded thinkers.

After school, many of us enter the working world, which is another big change to shape of thinking and develop our feelings. The workplace is very different from school and our home environment. We use our knowledge in practical ways, often under pressure, learning that there are certain experiences and how we process information is not in textbook or from what we learn at home. Work ethics become crucial. Being on time, responsible, and reliable are not just good qualities, but expectations that are necessary. We quickly learn about consequences that can occur when we fail to meet certain expectations, developing how we think and feel.

In the workplace, we learn to balance different aspects of our lives. We manage work, family, and personal interests. We also develop professional skills. We learn to work in teams, manage projects, and communicate effectively. These skills are vital for success in any career.

The workplace also teaches us about the world and the demands that comes from wanting more and pursuing to excel. We learn about different industries, markets, and global trends. We understand how businesses work and how they contribute to society. We also learn about the challenges and opportunities in our field. Our thoughts and thinking patterns continue to evolve as we move through life. Each stage - home, school, and work - adds new layers to our thinking. We learn from our experiences and from the people we meet. This lifelong learning shapes who we are and how we see the world.

Our minds are shaped by many things developing our things of what we think of ourselves, others and certain challenges we encounter in life. Our thoughts come from the world around us, our culture, family, education, work, friends, and personal choices influence our thinking. By understanding these influences, we can understand ourselves better.

Let's look closer at some of these influences. Culture plays a big role. The values and beliefs we grow up with impact our worldview. What people around us think is normal, which shapes our perspective. The media we consume also influences our thinking. The culture we're immersed in is like the air we breathe. We may not notice it, but it shapes our thoughts.

Our families are another influence. Parents, siblings, and relatives teach us ways of seeing things. Family traditions create habits of thinking we carry through life. The way our family talks about events, other cultures, ethnicity, and how we interpret things makes a different in how we think. Warm, supportive families can instill confidence and open-mindedness. Difficult family situations can also shape our thoughts to either become better or consider it as a "normal" way of life. Either way, families have a deep influence on our minds and how we think.

Friends and social circles widen our lens further. Spending time with different types of people introduces us to new worldviews. Casual conversations, deep discussions, and shared experiences all shape our thoughts. Relationships exercise our emotional intelligence. They fine-tune our ability to communicate, cooperate, and compromise.

Beyond these influences, our personal choices direct our thinking which can affect our feelings. The goals we pursue, media we consume, and how we spend our free time - these actively shape our mental landscape. Our unique interests, curiosities, and values filter what we absorb. Even when facing the same situations as others, we each perceive things in our own way. Our inner voice makes meaning from experiences depending on how we shape our thinking.

Navigating these many influences is key to growth. With discipline, we can focus our thinking and not get distracted, providing they can bring fruitfulness to our lives. We can reflect on our beliefs and change what no longer serves us to avoid regrets and past negative experiences. By picking our battles, we avoid wasting energy on trivial issues. Lifelong learning keeps our minds open, fresh and adaptable, especially when we can see the light at the end of the tunnel. Staying persistent to think positive and optimistic regardless of the challenges we encounter will change our mood and keep us happy.

There will always be challenges that test our thinking. Ethical dilemmas cannot be solved by simple formulas. Making sound decisions requires weighing many interlocking factors. Solving complex problems needs knowledge from different fields to see the full picture, and this will come with maturity. The past experience we gain from shaping our minds and how we look at things deepens our judgment and helps us to be less worried.

Our thoughts go through ups and downs just like life. Achieving goals can fill us with confidence and capability. But mistakes and setbacks, though painful, contain lessons that refine our thinking. Our roles at work and home grow and evolve as we do. Each phase of life reshapes our perspective and how we think makes a vast difference.

To conclude, our unique mix of influences creates our distinctive way of thinking. By shaping our influences from our home, family, school, work and the world around us, we shape our minds and how we think. We can transform fixed mindsets into growth mindsets. With self-awareness, we can upgrade habits that no longer serve us. Although we cannot control everything, we have great power to cultivate our thoughts.

We need to remind ourselves that our minds contain multitudes of thoughts from any and everything we go through in life. Thoughts have remarkable depth, breadth and beauty depending on if we shape them to be more positive than negative. They make life profoundly meaningful as we experience what healthy thinking can lead to. Our inner world governs so much of how we experience outer reality. Understanding the origins of our thinking is the starting point. This knowledge helps us take charge of our minds and unlock our vast potential. Our journey of thought never ends. And that is what makes it so rewarding.

# Chapter 1 The Origins Of Thought

Chapter 2

# The Intricacies of Thought Processes

People's minds are astoundingly busy places, almost like bustling marketplaces where thoughts of every variety vie for attention. On average, between 20,000 to 70,000 thoughts cross human minds each day, ranging from mundane matters like what to have for breakfast to profound philosophical musings. This constant mental activity is both natural and universal regardless of culture and ethnicity. When we think that our minds are overly active or our thoughts are too chaotic, it's essential to remember that this is a universal human experience.

From the time we were born, our surroundings start to shape the way we think. Our brains are very flexible when we are young children, it's like a sponge that absorbs everything including wanted and unwanted information. This allows change and growth to be natural. Because young brains are so flexible, the things that happen during childhood have a big impact on how we learn, feel, and act as we age. This important time is called the "critical window" or "windows of growth."

## Chapter 2 The Intricacies Of Thought Processes

The family has the earliest and biggest effect on children's brains. When parents or caregivers meet children's needs, they feel safe. This helps them build strong emotional bonds or "attachment" to caregivers. Secure bonds as babies make it easier to have good relationships and create maturity in how to think. How parents act shapes children's views of marriage and how couples get along.

As discussed in the first chapter, education in the school system are the next biggest influence to shaping how we see ourselves and how we view others. It is during this period mental health issues arises leading from mental health traits to a formal diagnosis when not cared for. This is the time when personality disorders are developed. The education system teaches how our society operates and how vicious and selfish people can be. We learn what people expect from us and how to meet demands. Intelligence grows as curiosity develops. We learn about interests, opinions, and open-or closed-mindedness that can stays with us as adults.

Work teaches professional ethics and skills for specific careers which can affect what co-workers say and do. It pushes people to adapt their thinking to workplace needs. Offices and job sites expose employees to diverse views. This requires flexible thinking. Leadership, teamwork, handling conflicts, and coping with stress are skills improved at work.

Beyond family, school, and work, broader society influences what we think and how we implement what we have processed in our thoughts. Cultural norms define good and bad behaviour and values. Religious beliefs often guide moral choices and gives us a sense of hope when we experience the value of positive thinking. Culture and faith provide a framework for individuals' thoughts.

Self-discipline, whether learned from society or oneself, structures our many thoughts. It helps focus on actions that match values and goals. This shapes the future, and we think about ourselves, others, education and what we study, work diligently, or live healthily fine-tunes thoughts to produce wanted results.

Understanding how our thoughts develop, helps us to understand people line of thinking, their behaviours think and why they act the way they do. We learn the concept of not trying to "fix" a person but rather how to accommodate them.

Self-discipline's structures enable focus on goals, values, and helpful behaviours in supporting ourselves from unnecessary stress. We learn finding solutions is necessary to move ahead, but we are not obligated to find answers for every else's problem. We prioritize useful actions to shape a positive future, molding constructive thought patterns that brings growth and maturity. Appreciating these influences grants insight into building beneficial mindsets and achieving personal growth.

**Thoughts Shape Reality**

Each person has their own unique thoughts and beliefs. These shape who we are and what we do. If we believe we are good at a certain area of life, a hobby, talent, or business we put all our energy towards it with hope to become experts. Like a young student who believes they are good at math, they will likely try hard in math class. They will spend time working on tough math problems and will get excited to learn new things in math. Over time, their belief in being good at math can come true where their career may lead to a job in finances, engineering, chemistry etc. This shows how our thoughts about ourselves develop into a passion that creates a happy future. This does not mean we will be eliminated from issues along the way because we are good at something or striving to be good in an area, we can be expert in. But rather we will not allow out thoughts to go down the ribbit hole where we sit in darkness because things are not working out.

Maturity in our thinking will look for solutions and not put on a self-blaming attitude or blaming others. When we condition our minds to be positive and restructure how we think we will see more of a positive outcome.

People think in many different ways. This makes humanity interesting and diverse. But there are also some common ways of thinking in groups.

## Chapter 2 The Intricacies Of Thought Processes

These are the normal ethics, culture, and laws in a society. They guide what people see as okay to think and do where they live. But "normal" changes between different places and times. What seems normal in one culture may seem very strange in another.

For example, in some societies today it's typical for young adults to move away from their parents' home. They get their own apartment in a new city. But a few generations ago, it was more common for families to live together their whole lives. No one way is right or wrong. It depends on the beliefs and values of that time and place. The changes to societal thinking can create negative thoughts if individuals are not willing to adapt.

The same goes for how we see ourselves. Maybe you grew up thinking it was normal to follow a certain career path like your parents. But your own interests and talents may actually fit a very different profession. If you only do what seems "normal," you won't explore your full potential. This can create regrets in life as to why you did not choose what was best for your instead of what you parents wanted. On the other hand, an individuals can also have regrets from not following in the legacy of their parents hoping their choice would have been the best one.

Whatever choice you make in life, embrace it and not to allow your mind to take you into a regret place. Your negative thoughts will develop creating mental health issues to develop and when untreated it can formulate into a disorder.

As the world changes, so do our collective ways of thinking. Things that were once seen as unacceptable become more accepted over time. More people feel safe to be themselves in public. There is more understanding for people of different backgrounds. Of course, there are still many challenges. Prejudices pass from one generation to the next. Habits of thought are not easy to change. But the trend shows society gradually expanding our minds forcing us to think different.

There is a generation before us and after us and they all think different. You have to take what is applicable to you in your generation to avoid negativity to creep into you mind. There will always be the good, the bad and the ugly, you choose without pointing fingers and allowing you conscience to hunt your with negative thinking.

Progress comes when people think for themselves while also caring for others. We consider our own needs and don't just blindly conform. At the same time, we try to understand what others go through. Open and ethical thinking creates hope for the future, just like opening the mind with everything that is thrown your way. It takes work from all of us, every day, to get to a place where we are comfortable and can have healthy thoughts.

**No "Right" or "Wrong": The Relativity of Thought**

Thinking that there is no "right" or "wrong" way to think challenges many cultures, religions, and ethics. These systems often separate thoughts into "good" and "bad". But thoughts themselves are neutral. They are like clay waiting to be shaped. The question is not whether thoughts are good or bad. It is how people use, understand, and act on them.

Modern psychology and brain science show thoughts are neutral. In the brain, thoughts are connections between neurons. These connections make patterns whether society sees the patterns as "right" or "wrong" depends on other things. These include social rules, moods, and morals. For example, feeling angry is normal just like feeling happy or sad. The feeling is activated by a thought and how we act on the thoughts has an outcome that can be positive or negative.

Thoughts depend on culture, society, and personal background. One culture may find some thoughts virtuous. Another culture may frown on those same thoughts. Take individualism and community, for example. In some Western societies, thoughts about personal freedom and independence are valued highly. Many Eastern cultures focus more on family and community duties. Neither view is inherently "right" or "wrong." They show different ways of life shaped by history, geography, and culture.

Ethics and morals often guide how thoughts turn into actions. The thoughts themselves remain neutral. But the actions they lead to can be right or wrong according to ethical rules. It is important to separate the thought from the action. For example, briefly thinking about stealing does not make someone a thief, it crosses an ethical line.

Thoughts are neutral and shaped by many outside factors. So they can change. By noticing unhelpful thought patterns and questioning them, people can "rewire" their brains to think differently. This shows the brain's flexibility. Rather than labeling thoughts as "bad" and trying to bury them, it is better to understand where they come from and whether they are useful.

In conclusion, the relativity of thoughts gives people great power. They can use thoughts to grow, learn, and help others or they can use thoughts destructively, harming themselves and others. Thoughts can build a fulfilling life or continue cycles of despair.

By embracing the many thoughts that come each day, realizing what has shaped them, understanding the power of beliefs, and considering cultural ethics, people gain a deeper view of their thinking. This understanding is the base for an intentional, fulfilling life.

# Fantasy and Reality Thinking

Navigating the complexities of the human mind involves acknowledging two overlapping yet distinct domains: fantasy and reality. These domains not only contribute to the richness of human experience but also shape the strategies people employ to cope with life's challenges and pursue its opportunities. By examining the interplay between these two realms, a more comprehensive understanding of human cognition and behaviour can be achieved.

We all have dreams, fantasies, and reality thinking. What affects our thinking is when we are not able to see growth in the choices we make. Some of us may choose to live in a fantasy world as there is no expectations to live up to. The emotional pain has created a mind to live in a numb mode where only dreaming creates peace.

**The Genesis of Fantasy: Dreams, Visions, and Goals**

From the time children become aware of the world around them, their minds start to imagine things that are not really there. They like to pretend they are conquering mythical kingdoms or exploring undiscovered planets. This is more than just playing around. It sets the foundation for a

## Chapter 3 Fantasy And Reality Thinking

lifelong relationship with dreams, visions, and goals. As children learn about the world, this flexible thinking lets them adapt, learn, and grow in ways that would not be possible without the ability to see things not just as they are, but also as they could be.

Dreams and visions play a central role in mental health and feeling good emotionally. Pretending lets children escape the stresses of everyday life. The ability to dream gives the mind a break from immediate worries. This lets the mind have time it needs to come up with new ideas, solve problems, or simply rest. This type of escape, when not overdone, makes people more resilient. It helps them feel steady emotionally and manage stress.

At a deeper level, these fantasies can turn into life goals. For example, a teenager who dreams of becoming a doctor might take real steps to make this vision happen. They could get excellent grades in school or volunteer at a healthcare facility. This change from the imaginary to the real shows the transformative power of dreams and visions when they become targeted goals.

Understanding the brain science behind imagining reveals complex thinking processes and neural activity. Specific areas of the brain, like the default mode network, become active when people daydream or envision the future. This network interacts with other systems for executive function and emotional control. Together they form a unified mental picture of someone's dreams and aims.

Culture, family, and social norms deeply affect the kinds of dreams and goals people seek. In some cultures, the focus might be on community values, steering dreams toward communal success and family honour. By contrast, individualistic societies might encourage more personalized goals like individual achievement and self-fulfillment. Understanding this social layer is vital for grasping how dreams and visions are shaped by larger outside forces, not just personal choices.

As people mature, their dreams, visions, and goals mature too. Early dreams of becoming an astronaut may change into a passion for aerospace engineering or dedication to scientific research. Or they may transform completely, directed now toward the arts or social sciences. But the basic ability to dream and picture various possible futures stays the same. It serves as a guide through the winding paths of life's possibilities.

However, the realm of fantasy is not without risks. Constant daydreaming could lead to ignoring responsibilities or losing touch with real consequences. Individuals who may be suffering with psychosis may confuse their reality with a fantasy as they lose touch with reality. Their normal becomes abnormal of society.

More broadly, the nature and scope of one's dreams may involve ethical implications. For example, the drive to succeed no matter what could compromise moral character. It could lead to choices that negatively affect others. So while dreams drive achievement and happiness, they must align with ethical standards and social duties.

Imagination allows children to envision the world not just as it is, but also as it could be. As they grow, dreams can evolve into targeted goals and steps toward achievement. A capacity for healthy fantasy promotes resilience and emotional well-being. However, unchecked fantasizing carries risks, so dreams must be pursued ethically. Overall, imagination and vision serve a vital role in mental health, motivation, and navigating life's possibilities.

**The Risks and Causes of Escapism**

Escaping from life's problems is complicated. It involves many layers and comes from deep inside us. While it's normal to want to get away from trouble, how much we use this to cope can greatly affect our mental health, relationships, and overall wellbeing. To understand the good, the bad and the ugly parts of escaping, we need to look closely at why and how it happens.

At its core, escaping gives us another reality that seems better than our real life. Whether it's daydreams, video games, drugs or alcohol, an easier, simpler world can be very tempting. But this appeal often hides the

## Chapter 3 Fantasy And Reality Thinking

risks. When the fantasy world becomes more attractive than the real one, and hours turn to days lost in it, warning bells should go off. Escaping becomes dangerous when it replaces engaging with life, stopping personal growth, hurting relationships, and even risking health.

Stress, worry, mental illness, the misuse of medications, alcohol, illicit drugs, cannabis and cognitive issues like negative thinking can all create escaping from reality. It causes isolation from reality leading to psychological issues.

One of the most worrying forms of escape is substance abuse. The artificial highs of drugs or alcohol may briefly escape life's troubles but at a huge cost. Depending on substances can destroy physical health, impair judgment, and start an addiction cycle that's very hard to break. Also, drugs, cannabis use and alcohol can dramatically change how the brain works, making it even harder to deal with the underlying issues that made someone want to escape in the first place.

Escaping isn't always about imaginary worlds or numbing the mind with substances; sometimes it's emotional detachment. People may distance themselves from friends, family, duties, and activities that require mental or emotional investment. While less obviously destructive than substance abuse, emotional detachment can still have long-term consequences, including damaged relationships and neglecting responsibilities key to personal and professional growth.

Escaping often comes from deeper, unresolved problems like past trauma, current stress, dissatisfaction with life, or mental health issues such as depression or anxiety. People may also escape to cope with feelings of failure, guilt, or immense pressure from work, family, or social expectations. Recognizing these root causes is the first step to healthier coping.

Noticing when escaping goes from natural coping to potentially harmful behaviour is crucial for changing course. Awareness is the first part of breaking the cycle. Consulting mental health professionals can provide valuable insight into why someone escapes excessively and offer effective strategies that address the root problems rather than just the symptoms.

Escaping provides both refuge and potential prison. While it can temporarily relieve life's stresses and disappointments, relying too much on escape can cause many compounding problems over time. Understanding the risks and recognizing the underlying causes is key to maintaining a healthy balance between imagination's flights of fancy and grounding realities.

**Reality Thinking: The Grounding Force**

Thinking about reality acts like an anchor for the mind, while fantasizing serves as its compass. Reality thinking means clearly seeing the world as it is. It relies on logic and facts. This kind of thinking allows people to do everyday things, solve problems, and connect with others in a meaningful way. While fantasizing does not offer the same emotional comfort, reality thinking gives people the tools to take on life's challenges directly.

Observing the world empirically and using logic to make deductions helps people make informed choices. This critical foundation allows for scientific discoveries, running businesses, and managing relationships. Reality thinking also involves self-awareness. It lets people recognize their own limitations, evaluate their abilities, and plan accordingly.

The main challenge is finding a balance between fantasy and reality thinking. Fantasizing can provide creative fuel for innovation and emotional support for mental well-being. But it needs to connect to reality to produce tangible results. On the other hand, focusing too much on reality thinking could limit creativity. It could also make it harder to envision a future different from the present.

Striking the right balance is like walking a tightrope. On one side, there is the risk of getting so caught up in fantasy that you lose touch with reality. This could lead to ignoring responsibilities or more serious psychological problems. On the other side, there is the risk of staying so anchored in the present reality that you resist change, innovation or personal growth.

Reality thinking starts with gathering information through our five senses - sight, hearing, taste, touch, and smell. We use our powers of observation to take in details about the world around us. Then logic and reasoning come into play as we analyze the raw data from our senses. Step-by-step, we make connections and identify patterns to form conclusions based on the evidence.

This process of inductive and deductive reasoning is the essence of reality thinking. We make general inferences from specific examples. Then we test our hypotheses and modify them based on the results. Each small deduction builds gradually toward larger theories and principles. Scientific methods formalize this approach, but we use the same basic thought processes in our everyday lives.

Reality thinking helps us in practical ways. It allows us to navigate from place to place by understanding directions. It helps us avoid dangers by assessing risks and acting accordingly. We can make well-informed choices about careers, finances, relationships and more by researching options and weighing pros and cons. Reality thinking is crucial for accomplishing goals, whether it's following a recipe, assembling furniture, or developing a business plan.

On the other hand, fantasy thinking is free from the constraints of reality. It allows our imagination to wander beyond the limits of what we can directly see, hear, taste, touch, and smell. Fantasy provides a canvas where anything is possible, unbound from rules, facts, or logic. It lets our creative spirit soar.

In conclusion, fantasy, and reality thinking work together dynamically to impact how people navigate life. Both are essential and have benefits and downsides. Understanding how to use them effectively could be the key to a fulfilling life.

Learn to dream big and allow your imagination to go wild, and then explore options as to what can be done to bring those dreams to reality. Anything is possible when you put your mind to it. The dance between fantasy and reality is a core part of human experience and we have the power to choose.

# Chapter 3 Fantasy And Reality Thinking

## Chapter 4

# Why Do I Think More Negative Thoughts Than Positive Ones?

We are programmed for survival, not happiness, which might explain why our brains have a natural tendency to focus on the negative aspects of life. The emotional weight of a negative experience often lingers longer than that of a positive one, offering a fascinating yet complex topic to understand. Why do some of us lean more heavily toward negative thinking? The answer often involves an intricate interplay of various factors.

Negative thinking can often be traced back to a foundational belief: the absence of self-belief. If individuals don't believe they can achieve their goals or overcome challenges, the motivation to try diminishes, resulting in a self-fulfilling prophecy of failure and, consequently, more negative thinking.

**Insecurities**

## Chapter 4 Why Do I Think More Negative Thoughts Than Positive Ones?

Insecurity can distort how we see ourselves, like a funhouse mirror that stretches or shrinks aspects of who we are. These distorted views often come from early experiences, like childhood trauma or critical parents. They can also come from social media, where comparing ourselves to others makes us feel inadequate. Past failures or rejections can also plant seeds of insecurity deep inside us.

Once they take root, insecurities create a cycle of negative thinking and self-doubt. For example, someone who feels insecure about their intelligence might stay quiet in group discussions. They worry about being judged or ridiculed. By not participating, they reinforce their insecurity. It can even lead to poor performance that further grows their self-doubt.

In relationships, insecurities show up as jealousy, neediness and constantly seeking validation. The fear of not being "enough" makes people hypersensitive to any perceived criticism from partners/spouses, friends, or colleagues. This sensitivity strains relationships and becomes a self-fulfilling prophecy. The act of constantly seeking reassurance can drive others away, proving the original insecurity right.

Insecurities also impact physical health. Constant anxiety about not measuring up leads to issues like sleep problems or cardiovascular disease. Insecurities may also drive unhealthy habits like overeating, addictions, substance abuse or obsessive exercise. These compromise our well-being even further.

Overcoming insecurity is an ongoing process that often requires self-reflection, behaviour changes and sometimes professional help. We need to identify these harmful thought patterns and replace them with more positive beliefs. Building a strong support system, practicing self-compassion and setting achievable goals also help fight the distortions insecurity causes.

In the big picture, insecurities are one part of complex human psychology. However, their ability to shape perceptions, dictate behaviours and affect well-being makes them powerful. While they may never fully disappear, understanding insecurities is the first step toward reducing their impact. It helps steer life in a more positive, fulfilling direction.

Insecurity stems from a lack of self-confidence and self-esteem. We may question our own abilities, talents or worthiness of love. Even highly accomplished individuals can struggle with insecurity. It often comes from deeper issues like low self-worth or fear of failure.

Insecurities hold us back from reaching our full potential. They fill our minds with self-limiting beliefs and negative self-talk. Statements like "I'm not good enough" or "I don't deserve this" undermine our ability to succeed. Insecurity creates a mental framework of doubt, uncertainty and hesitation.

This mindset affects how we approach challenges. Insecure people avoid risk-taking so they won't have to face potential failure or judgment. They downplay their talents so expectations won't be too high. They hold back from pursuing big goals, convincing themselves "I could never do that." Insecurity is paralyzing.

In relationships, insecurity rears its head through neediness and jealousy. Insecure individuals constantly seek validation from others. They need frequent reassurance they are loved. This clinginess often suffocates relationships. Insecurity also fuels irrational jealousy over harmless interactions. No amount of reassurance relieves the doubt.

Insecurity even impacts physical health. Chronic stress and anxiety from feeling inadequate take a toll. Insomnia, headaches, weight gain and high blood pressure can result. Insecurity may also drive unhealthy coping mechanisms like substance abuse, eating disorders or obsessive exercise.

Overcoming insecurity requires slowly replacing self-doubt with self-belief. Building genuine self-confidence takes time. We need to identify our triggers. What experiences or situations spark insecurity? Avoiding or managing triggers reduces their power.

Challenge negative thoughts. When insecure beliefs creep in, consciously replace them with a more positive perspective. Celebrate small wins — achieving little goals reinforces capabilities. Give yourself credit for each one. Take risks. Do something that scares you every day, even if small. Face fear and build self-assurance.

Seek support. Confide in trusted friends and family. Their belief in you helps drown out the negative self-talk. Be kind to yourself. Insecurity often stems from harsh self-criticism. Treat yourself with compassion.

With consistent effort, insecurity's grip will slowly loosen. Self-confidence grows each time we overcome fear, achieve a goal or quiet the inner critic. Progress builds momentum.

In the end, insecurity is part of being human. Even the most successful people have moments of doubt. The key is not eliminating insecurity completely, but managing it. Identify when it holds you back, then push forward anyway. Each small step forward brings you closer to realizing your full potential.

**Lack of Confidence**

Lack of confidence is a common struggle that many people face. Even though confidence seems like something you either have or don't have, it's actually more complex than that. Lack of confidence isn't just an absence of confidence - it's an active force that shapes how we think, act, and live our lives.

Imagine you walk into a room and feel like everyone is judging you. You think they're critiquing what you're wearing, how you styled your hair, the way you're talking, even the way you're breathing. It's like there's a spotlight on only you, showing all your flaws for everyone to see. Lack of confidence is the director of this uneasy show, making you feel like you're always being examined but never measuring up. This outlook doesn't disappear when you leave the room either. It continues to impact you in different situations, making even simple tasks seem incredibly difficult.

When you lack confidence, every job interview feels like an interrogation. Each social interaction becomes a performance that will be critiqued. Every decision seems like a potential catastrophe waiting to happen. With this limiting mindset, negative feedback isn't a tool for growth - it's confirmation of your worst fears. On the flip side, any positive feedback is doubted, attributed to *"luck"* or other's low expectations, but never your own skills or efforts. It's like you're going through life with a script in your head saying you're going to fail, so why even try?

There are a few potential reasons someone might lack confidence. Sometimes it stems from early life when caregivers were overly critical or teachers focused on weaknesses rather than strengths. In other cases, it could come from society praising certain attributes you feel you don't have. A string of setbacks or failures can also lead to generalizing that you're inadequate.

The physical aspect is important too. A brain constantly exposed to stress hormones like cortisol may find it harder to access positive, self-affirming thoughts. This hormonal state, often caused by the chronic stress lack of confidence induces, only strengthens neural pathways for self-doubt and insecurity. It creates a biochemical cycle as strong as any habit.

Despite its power, lack of confidence is not unavoidable. It's more like a story constructed over time, and like any story, it can be rewritten. The first step is recognizing the narrative exists, seeing how it was authored not just by you, but also your environment, experiences, and even biochemistry.

By challenging negative beliefs and distorted thinking patterns that feed lack of confidence, we can start reframing experiences in a more balanced, less judgmental way. We can practice awareness of the present moment, providing a break from the constant cycle of worry and self-doubt.

**Low Self-Esteem**

## Chapter 4 Why Do I Think More Negative Thoughts Than Positive Ones?

From an early age, some people develop low self-esteem. This can happen when parents only show love if the child succeeds. For these children, affection means being "the best". Even if families are supportive, unrealistic standards from society or peers can cause problems. Picture a teen trying to fit in on social media, where everyone looks perfect. Meanwhile, their own life feels messy and full of mistakes. With influences like these, low self-esteem can take root at a young age.

Once established, low self-esteem leads to constant self-criticism. Imagine walking into a room and feeling like you're under a spotlight. But instead of fame, the light reveals your flaws. Every step seems wrong. Every word sounds incorrect. It's like having a biased critic in your head who only notices the bad and ignores the good in your life.

Living with low self-esteem is like keeping a ship harboured indefinitely. It seems safer to avoid the unknown waters of life. Fear of failure or judgment weighs down the anchor. But by avoiding risks, you also miss out on adventures and growth. The ship stays still, not because of storms, but because the captain has lost faith in their skills.

Low self-esteem also affects relationships. Imagine believing you're unworthy of kindness. You see every nice gesture as charity and every insult as proof of your flaws. You desperately want validation from others, yet fear exposes the "real" you. It's a catch-22 of needing approval while expecting rejection.

The effects of low self-esteem extend beyond thoughts and feelings. People with low self-confidence often slouch, avoid eye contact, and speak softly. Sadness and anxiety frequently accompany a negative self-image, creating a loop of bad feelings that reinforce low self-worth.

But there is hope. With commitment and courage, the ship can still sail. The first step is acknowledging room for growth. Perfection is impossible; everyone makes mistakes. Expecting flawlessness only leads to disappointment and self-blame. Progress, not perfection, should be the goal.

We need to identify and challenge our negative self-talk. When the inner critic attacks, imagine talking to a friend instead. Would you condemn them as harshly? Treat yourself with the compassion you'd show another. Make a daily list of positive qualities, talents, and achievements. This trains your mind to recognize self-worth.

Open up to supportive loved ones. Vulnerability builds intimacy. Focus on being authentic, not obtaining approval. Share feelings and ask for encouragement, not criticism. Good relationships are built on empathy, not judgment. Surround yourself with people who reinforce your strengths.

Take small risks outside your comfort zone. Each success, however minor, is proof you can handle uncertainty. With every risk taken, the self-doubt loosens its grip. Give yourself credit for trying, regardless of the outcome. Failure is part of growth; it doesn't define you.

Make self-care a priority, not a luxury. Treat your body and mind with compassion through healthy habits. Get enough sleep, nutrition and exercise. Make time for hobbies and interests. Do things just because they bring joy, not external validation. You are worthy simply because you exist.

With consistent effort, the chains of low self-esteem can be broken. The path requires courage, patience and self-love. There will be setbacks, but don't abandon ship. Every small step forward is progress. Your life's adventure is waiting. You have the strength and ability to navigate it. The time is now to set sail.

**Pride and Ego**

Pride, when pure, lifts people up. It makes them feel good about what they've done. It reminds them they have talent and worth. Pride is like a big brother or sister. It pushes you to stand tall when life gets hard. But pride has a dark side too. It won't admit mistakes or take criticism. Pride changes from protector to stubborn gatekeeper. It fiercely guards an image of yourself that may be wrong. This stiff pride sets you up to fail.

## Chapter 4 Why Do I Think More Negative Thoughts Than Positive Ones?

No one's perfect, after all. Each mistake or insult hurts your pride more. It smudges your self-view and leads to bad thoughts.

The ego works differently than pride. Think of it as the frame around a mirror. It shapes your identity subtly but strongly. The ego helps you navigate social settings. But it craves drama, comparisons, and pats on the back. With a big ego, life's a stage and everyone's your critic. This drains you and stresses you out.

Oddly, the bigger the ego, the easier it bruises. Like an over-inflated balloon, small pricks pop it fast. A coworker's comment or a tiff with a loved one swiftly deflate it. This leads to bad thoughts or self-harm in some cases.

Handling pride and ego takes insight. We need to become aware that they exist and will sway us. Once aware, use them to build a fair self-image. Don't let them warp reality.

Sometimes, life feeds negativity too. Excessive control from parents, bosses, or partners/spouses breeds helplessness. You feel your actions don't affect your life. This cascades into negative thinking.

Personality plays a role as well. Introverts tend to brood over the past and fret about the future. Extroverts get down when social life disappoints. But introversion or extroversion isn't inherently bad. It's the unhealthy extremes that breed negativity.

Other things can also spur negative thinking. Social media often makes people feel inadequate. Seeing carefully curated glimpses of friends' lives can skew perspective. It leads to false comparisons about looks, success, and happiness. Too much screen time also reduces in-person interactions. This can worsen mood and self-image.

The mind instinctively focuses on threats and problems. Our ancestors who worried about predators and food shortages survived. But today this negativity bias backfires. Dwelling on modern worries just stresses you out.

We often personalize events too. We think everything relates to us closely. But many things have little to do with us. Recognizing this helps limit self-blame and angst when bad stuff happens.

Past traumas can also pollute thinking. Painful events cast shadows long after they occur. Feelings of helplessness or grief may linger. Working to process and resolve these feelings helps prevent ongoing gloom.

Chemistry impacts thinking too. Brain changes due to depression, anxiety, and other conditions can darken outlooks. Correcting chemical imbalances alleviates their effects.

Lifestyle habits also sway thinking. Lack of sleep, poor diet, not exercising, and increased substance use all breed negativity. Self-care lifts mood and self-worth.

Finally, words shape thoughts. Internal dialogues affect emotions powerfully. Notice negative self-talk when it arises. Replace it consciously with affirming messages.

The propensity for negative thinking can arise from a multitude of factors, often working in tandem to reinforce each other. Whether stemming from deep-rooted insecurities, environmental factors, or certain personality traits, understanding the source of one's negativity is the first step toward addressing it. With appropriate self-awareness and intervention, breaking free from the grip of persistent negative thoughts is an achievable goal.

# Chapter 4 Why Do I Think More Negative Thoughts Than Positive Ones?

# Chapter 5

# Thoughts are Affected by Beliefs - The Intrinsic Web of Mindset

Our minds are a complex mechanism that constantly processes information, emotions, and experiences. Among its many facets, one stands out for its ability to shape nearly every aspect of life: belief. What we believe deeply influences our thinking patterns, often in ways that are so subtle, they escape immediate notice. Yet, these beliefs have the power to build or destroy, to heal or to harm, making our understanding a vital endeavour.

**Beliefs in Personal Superiority**

When we start to believe that we are better than others, this thought can take over our minds. It becomes like glasses that colour how we see everything that happens to us. It's as if our lives are a play where we are both the actor and the audience, always trying to get praise and approval. This way of thinking does not just change our private thoughts. It also

## Chapter 5 Thoughts Are Affected By Beliefs - The Intrinsic Web Of Mindset

does not change how we act with other people. The energy we use to keep this belief alive means we often compare ourselves to others and compete with them. Every discussion becomes a way to prove we are superior and get respect. Conversations become more about winning than understanding.

But needing others to tell you that you are great all the time can become a problem. It can make you lonely, because you reduce the complexity of human interaction down to just getting validation. At work, believing you are superior can hurt teamwork, reduce empathy, and limit communication. This can lead to missed chances and strained relationships. In personal relationships, the need to be seen as better than others can override the need for love, connection, and mutual growth. In this way, the belief cuts both ways - it may briefly make you feel like a winner, but the cost is meaningful bonds and developing as a person.

Rather than comparing ourselves to others, we can focus on being the best version of ourselves. Every person has unique talents and gifts to offer. If we can recognize our own strengths as well as those of others, we create an environment where everyone can thrive. Mutual understanding, not constant competition, paves the path to fulfillment.

When we open our minds to learn from each other, we expand our horizons. Varied perspectives challenge us to grow. Through open and honest communication, we build trust. By lifting each other up, we all rise higher. Instead of limiting our interactions to superficial point-scoring, we can foster meaningful connections that enrich our lives.

Focusing less on validation frees us to pursue excellence on our own terms. We can channel energy into developing our talents, following our purpose, and leaving a positive mark on the world. Recognition may come, but it is a by-product, not the end goal. Our own growth and the service we provide become their own rewards.

**Lack of a Student Mind**

Learning is a lifelong journey. As we go through life, we constantly acquire new knowledge and skills. This helps us grow into better versions of ourselves. However, some people lose the desire to learn. They start believing that they have already learned everything they need to know. This false belief prevents them from growing further.

When someone thinks they know it all, they stop trying to improve. Their mind closes shut to new ideas and ways of thinking. This attitude hurts them badly in their career. At work, they resist learning new technologies and methods. They keep doing things the old way even when better options exist. This stagnation stalls their professional progress. As a result, their performance suffers over time, and they fail to reach their full potential.

Apart from careers, such a know-it-all attitude also damages personal relationships. People change with time, as do relationships. Failing to acknowledge and adapt to these changes, strains even the closest bonds. Friends may feel ignored or misunderstood due to poor communication. Romantic partners may drift apart over unresolved differences. Meaningful relationships require mutual growth and compromise. A rigid, unchanging mindset prevents this.

Beyond careers and relationships, a resistance to learn also restricts one's worldview. It narrows perspectives and entrenches prejudices. Life's inherent dynamism becomes lost on those who refuse to evolve with the changing times. Mental and emotional growth gets stunted. Dissatisfaction, aimlessness, and disconnection from society may follow.

In essence, the beliefs that we have learned enough or knows enough can profoundly limit our lives. We slam brakes on the natural human impulse for growth. Core beliefs like these, unless examined and corrected, can cost us our chances of fulfillment. We deprive ourselves of richer understanding, warm connections, and a deeper sense of purpose.

The good news is these beliefs can be overcome with awareness and effort. By recognizing their presence, we can consciously challenge them. We can reopen our minds to be lifelong students. Curiosity and humility can replace arrogance and intellectual laziness. When we embrace learning as a way of life, exciting possibilities open up. Our capabilities expand, and our perspectives broaden. Each day presents new lessons, experiences, and relationships.

**Allowing Personality and Character to Rule**

The way we think about ourselves has a big impact on our lives. If you believe that your personality and character cannot change, it will affect how your thoughts develop. This mindset creates a resistance to change and improvement. It's like your thoughts get stuck and cannot grow.

For example, if you firmly believe you are just plain 'bad at relationships,' that belief will shape your thoughts and actions when you are with other people. You expect to fail in relationships, so those negative expectations influence your experiences before they even happen. This kind of negative thinking can lead to a cycle where you only notice things that confirm your bad opinion of yourself.

Believing that your personality and character cannot change holds you back from growing as a person. It also causes problems in many areas of life. At work, you may feel unmotivated and lack ambition because you think you cannot improve. In relationships, you may have trouble opening up emotionally and building trust. Over time, believing you cannot change makes it very hard to actually change. It traps you in a maze of self-imposed limitations.

There are many downsides when someone assumes their personality is fixed. In their career, they may plateau early on and lose their drive to learn new skills. In social settings, they may isolate themselves due to fear of judgment. Romantic relationships suffer when someone is unable to be vulnerable. Mental health can decline when someone believes they are inherently anxious, depressed, or angry.

**Resistance to Change**

Change can be scary. We get comfortable in our routines and beliefs. When something threatens to shake up those routines or beliefs, it makes us uneasy. We want to cling to what we know.

New ideas that go against our current thinking create tension in our minds. We call this tension "cognitive dissonance." It is the discomfort we feel when new information conflicts with our existing beliefs. This discomfort comes from our desire to keep a stable view of the world.

To get rid of the discomfort, our minds try to avoid or explain away the new information. For example, we might tell ourselves the information is wrong or biased. Or we might try to fit the new idea into our old beliefs in a way that doesn't require us to change those beliefs much. By doing this, we can keep believing that our view of the world is consistent and unchanging, even when faced with evidence to the contrary.

Resisting change can hurt us in many areas of life. At work, refusing to update practices or learn new skills can make us less valuable employees. In relationships, not accepting growth and change in others can damage emotional bonds.

When we let our established mindsets rule our thinking, it's like we trap ourselves in a self-made prison. The familiarity of our beliefs brings some comfort and certainty. But resisting change also robs us of enriching experiences and personal growth.

To thrive, we must open ourselves to change, variety, and self-reflection. This takes courage. Examining our beliefs and assumptions can feel threatening. But leaning into discomfort is how we evolve and expand.

Embracing change involves risks. We may fail or feel embarrassed when trying something new. But the only real failure is allowing fear to stop our growth. With an open, growth-focused mindset, setbacks become opportunities to learn.

Progress requires stepping outside the comfort zones. People who actively challenge themselves reap the most rewards, professionally and personally. They are lifelong learners.

Two key habits can help us become more open-minded:

First, question your assumptions. Ask yourself why you believe what you do. Is it based on facts or feelings? Be willing to challenge long-held beliefs if new information suggests they may need updating.

Second, expose yourself to different people and ideas. Meet and listen to those outside your normal circles. Read broadly. Varied inputs spark creativity and growth.

With consistent practice, embracing change gets easier. Discomfort fades to excitement. Each leap builds courage for the next. Soon, you greet each new experience with curiosity rather than fear. The passion for growth becomes self-perpetuating.

This mindset propels personal fulfillment. Your world expands. You feel more creative, confident, and connected to others. By facing each moment as a fresh opportunity, you gain the flexibility and resilience to navigate life's twists and turns.

**Stuck in One's Generation**

The ability to adjust to changes between generations is important. When we cannot make this adjustment, our thinking stays locked in the norms and values we learned when we were young. Our thoughts are shaped by the past, which limits how we think now. This can cause problems connecting with the world today in many ways.

People who cannot adjust may have trouble with new technology, like using websites and apps on their phones. They may not understand younger people's views on politics, society, and relationships. When the world moves quickly but someone's mindset stays fixed in the past, they can feel left out and disconnected from society and even friends and family. Their old-fashioned viewpoint gets reinforced in their mind, making it hard to engage with the present.

This inflexibility has real impacts, especially at work where technology skills and adaptability are needed. Someone stuck in old ways of thinking may struggle with new communication methods, project tools, and data analysis expected by employers today. Socially, they may not understand terms, practices, and cultural trends that promote diversity and inclusion now. This makes it hard to connect meaningfully with people of different backgrounds.

Rather than judge or dismiss generational differences, an open mindset recognizes change is constant. While the past shapes who we are, holding on to it too tightly can limit growth. As the world evolves, we must gently expand our perspectives. With care and courage, we can bridge generational gaps and see that while surface behaviours and norms may change, our shared hopes and struggles remain.

Though learning new technologies may feel awkward at first, they open new possibilities. We can appreciate the fresh views of younger generations, even when they challenge our assumptions. And we can have patience with those who struggle to adapt, by listening without judgment and finding common ground. With compassion for ourselves and others, we can navigate changing times.

Progress need not wash away all we built and valued before. The new can complement old wisdom worth carrying forward. Our life stories stretch across generations, chapters of a greater human narrative. By honouring each chapter while turning the page, we craft truer understandings. Then doors once closed open to reveal our path ahead.

**Information Processing**

Our beliefs impact how we think. They act like filters that colour our view of information. These filters make the complex world simpler to understand. But they also skew our perceptions to match what we already believe. In this way, beliefs act like tinted glasses. They shade how we see things to reinforce our existing ideas.

## Chapter 5 Thoughts Are Affected By Beliefs - The Intrinsic Web Of Mindset

These biased filters shape thoughts across life. For example, confirmation bias leads people to focus on details that match their views. They ignore facts that contradict their beliefs. Also, the halo effect causes some individuals to highly value opinions of those they admire. This can lead to slanted perceptions that may not hold up logically. Biases particularly sway thoughts on big life choices like careers, relationships, or health.

Since biases stem from beliefs, which create a cycle. Existing beliefs get proven right over and over. This makes it difficult to see our flaws. Over time, the gap widens between how we see the world and reality. Eventually, our actions may not serve our best interests. Understanding how beliefs filter information becomes key for growth and objective choices.

Our beliefs powerfully impact how we interpret the world. While they can guide us through complexity, they can also blind us. Beliefs act as both compass and blinders. They point a direction but limit the view. Scrutinizing beliefs is not just an intellectual exercise. It is a vital step for personal growth and mental health.

To conclude, beliefs are like tinted glasses shading how we perceive information. Biases align new data with existing beliefs, creating a cycle of reinforcement. This can lead to a growing gap between our perceptions and reality over time. Recognizing how beliefs filter our thoughts is crucial for objective decision-making and growth. Examining our beliefs helps remove the blinders that may limit our vision and opportunities.

## Chapter 6

# Left Brain and Right Brain Thinker

Each person's brain is wired in their own special way. Even though we share most of our genes and culture, the small differences in how we think can lead to big differences in how we act, make choices, and see the world.

The brain is complex. It has about 86 billion brain cells connected together in complicated networks. These networks create our thoughts, feelings, and awareness. Even tiny differences in how the networks connect, shaped by both genetics and life experiences, can change how we think. This includes everything from solving problems and remembering things to controlling emotions and creative talents.

Science has mapped out the areas of the brain that handle different kinds of thinking. For example, the front part of the brain manages planning and decision-making. The amygdala handles emotional processing. But these areas don't work alone. They work together as a system to produce what we know as thinking.

## Chapter 6 Left Brain And Right Brain Thinker

How these areas connect can differ a lot between people. Many things shape these connections, like genes, childhood experiences, education, and social status. For instance, someone raised in a home that values academics and logic may develop stronger brain pathways for those skills. But someone else exposed to lots of art may build stronger creative and visual pathways.

Outside factors like culture and upbringing can strengthen these natural differences even more. Culture wires our brains through what skills it finds important and through its influence on language. Language, in turn, shapes thought and carry multiple words for concepts that other languages sum up in one word. This affects how speakers see and categorize the world.

Understanding our unique thinking style offers insights into our strengths and weaknesses. This allows personal growth by developing our abilities or improving weaker areas through practice or training.

Our diverse thinking styles also drive social progress. Different thinking allows people to approach problems in various ways, leading to more complete solutions. This is why teams of people from different backgrounds often find more innovative answers than homogeneous groups.

**Impact on Relationships**

Differences in how people think can greatly impact relationships. Accepting these differences helps people work together. This acceptance goes beyond just acknowledging differences. It means truly understanding how thinking styles complement each other. This benefits relationships, workplaces, schools, communities, and individuals.

In personal relationships, accepting different thinking styles lays the groundwork for respect and harmony. Some individuals may process information differently, and approach disagreements with openness, not accusations. And a creative thinker may not immediately understand detailed planning, but knowing their thinking diversity prompts collaboration, and not conflict.

At work, accepting different thinking styles optimizes performance. An organization that recognizes the strengths of creative and analytical thinkers can assign roles accordingly. Imagine a marketing team where analytical thinkers handle data and metrics. Creative thinkers develop content and interact with clients. This utilizes everyone's natural strengths, improving efficiency and innovation.

In schools, appreciating diverse learning styles creates an inclusive environment. Traditional education often favours analytical thinkers, marginalizing creative students. A balanced approach that values different skills engages more students. It develops a wider range of abilities.

In society, accepting cognitive diversity builds cohesion. It's easy to dismiss those who think differently as irrational or emotional. Recognizing thinking styles as different, not better or worse, promotes inclusivity. Community programs and political discussions benefit from diverse perspectives which leads to more balanced and effective solutions.

Individuals gain deeper self-understanding by accepting different thinking styles. Knowing how others think builds cognitive empathy. This allows more skillful social navigation, enriching relationships.

Appreciating diverse thinking styles positively impacts relationships, organizations, education, communities, and personal growth. Mutual understanding breeds collaboration, innovation, inclusivity, and social harmony. Accepting how we think differently is key to bringing out the best in ourselves and others.

## Strengths and Weaknesses of the Left-Brain Thinker and Right-Brain Thinker

Our brains let us do amazing things, from solving math puzzles to writing beautiful music. We often talk about "left-brain" and "right-brain" thinking to explain how our thoughts work. This is a simple way to understand different thinking styles, even though modern science shows

## Chapter 6 Left Brain And Right Brain Thinker

both sides of our brain work together. Looking at left-brain strengths and weaknesses gives us a useful model for logical thinking.

Those who lean on left-brain strengths are great at logic and reason. They excel at breaking down problems step-by-step to find solutions. It gives clear rules and defined parts, and they analyze each piece to get an answer. This skill is so valuable and precise, where measurable results matter. Fields like law, math, and engineering rely on following established rules to reach conclusions.

In social settings, left-brain thinkers take a level-headed approach to solving problems. They cut through messy emotions to find practical solutions. Their ability to think sequentially lets them outline plans and timelines efficiently. This makes them ideal for project management roles.

But this logical focus has limits. Left-brain thinkers can struggle with open-ended questions or vague situations. Creative tasks often need a more flexible mindset, which can be difficult for them. Their strict analytical framework means overlooking human factors that don't fit neatly into quantitative analysis. This can lead to misunderstandings in relationships since social cues don't align with their reasoning style.

Left-brain thinkers excel at academic subjects like science and math. Their skills help them break questions into organized, logical steps. But more abstract topics like art or ethics challenge their linear thinking. Their learning style favours concrete details over big-picture concepts. Hands-on activities tend to engage them more than group discussions or debates.

In the workplace, left-brain thinkers thrive when given well-defined responsibilities and expectations. They prefer direct instructions over vague directives. Their ability to create orderly processes and workflows makes them great at optimizing systems and procedures. But they may struggle to collaborate on undefined or creative projects.

In their personal life, these logical thinkers often have intense focus areas or hobbies. They devote great time and attention to mastering the precise rules of a game, instrument, or tool. But they may find it tiresome to make small talk or participate in group social gatherings. Their idea of fun is learning and analyzing, not wandering through abstract topics.

Left-brain tendencies have pros and cons. This thinking style lends itself to order, logic, and systematic analysis. But it comes up short when tasks require subjective or intuitive skills. The most effective thinkers integrate strengths from both sides of their brain. Logical reasoning blended with creative inspiration unlocks our greatest potential for discovery and achievement. Though the left brain prefers certainty, the ambiguity of life calls on us to adapt. Balancing analytical and imaginative thinking allows us to meet any challenge.

Right-brain thinkers on the other hand have many strengths that make them great at creative and emotional work. Their skills let them thrive in places where they can express themselves creatively and deal with complicated feelings. These talented people can understand and interpret emotions exceptionally well. They are also good at visual-spatial tasks like drawing and sculpting. Right-brain thinkers often have lively imaginations. This helps them see the big picture instead of getting stuck on small details. Their imaginative abilities make them wonderful at brainstorming sessions as they come up with many ideas.

In addition, right-brain thinkers are intuitive and can make connections between ideas that seem unrelated. This talent is invaluable for creative problem-solving. Their holistic thinking makes them a great fit for fields like psychology, marketing, or the arts where grasping human motivation and emotion is key.

However, the strengths of right-brain thinkers come with challenges. They may have trouble with tasks that require close attention to detail. It can also be difficult for them to bring structure to disorganized information. Additionally, their emotional sensitivity, while allowing them to navigate complex social situations, can lead to burnout especially in high-stress environments. In cases like these a more detached analytical approach would be beneficial.

## Chapter 6 Left Brain And Right Brain Thinker

In summary, right-brain thinkers excel in realms that involve creativity, emotions, and imagination. Their intuitive abilities aid in connecting disparate ideas and seeing the big picture. However, they struggle with details, organization, and emotional regulation in high-pressure situations. Recognizing these strengths and weaknesses allows right-brain thinkers to leverage their skills while developing strategies to overcome their challenges. With self-awareness, these creative and emotionally intelligent individuals can find roles where they can thrive and make unique contributions.

**Introversion and Extroversion**

The way our brains are organized relates interestingly to personality characteristics like being introverted or extroverted. For example, an introverted person who thinks mostly with the left side of their brain may like doing things alone that need deep focus and detailed analysis. They may find satisfaction in solving complicated math problems or writing computer code. On the other hand, an extroverted person who thinks mostly with the right side of their brain might enjoy social settings where they can have complex emotional interactions or come up with creative solutions in a group.

Being introverted or extroverted is not just about liking to be alone or be with others. It also affects how people process thoughts and feelings. An introvert may have long internal conversations with themselves before making a decision. An extrovert might look for external stimuli and other people's opinions as a way to test out their thoughts.

Understanding the complicated relationships between using the left or right brain and being introverted or extroverted gives us a richer view of our thinking. This view from multiple angles can inform everything from school and career choices to relationships and personal growth strategies.

For example, knowing that left-brain introverts thrive on solo activities requiring deep analysis could help someone choose a career involving mathematical research or computer programming over one centered on group creative projects. Or an extroverted right-brain thinker may better understand their desire to constantly seek out social stimulation and new collaborative endeavours rather than quiet contemplative pursuits.

Similarly, recognizing an introvert may require extensive internal processing before vocalizing thoughts can improve relationships with partners who operate differently. The extrovert can practice patience in allowing the introvert time and space to fully develop their perspectives before pressuring them to engage verbally. And the introvert can make an effort to occasionally share emerging thought processes to avoid seeming emotionally distant.

When it comes to education, some of us who use mostly left or right brain thinking may learn better through different teaching methods. A left-brain master's material best through logical sequences like mathematical proofs or grammar rules. A right-brain thrives when accessing creativity, imagination, and big picture concepts. If we are able to incorporate both analytic detail and creative engagement will reach more goals in life.

Understanding our own predominant brain orientation and personality traits allows tailoring personal growth strategies. A left-brain introvert may set a goal to improve public speaking skills by meticulously practicing speeches alone before ever going in front of an audience. An extroverted right-brain thinker's path includes improve classes and other unscripted interactions to become more comfortable with spontaneity.

To conclude, the interplay between brain hemisphere dominance and introversion versus extroversion provides insight into the diversity of our thinking and behaviour. Applying this knowledge allows optimization of education, careers, relationships and personal growth. By embracing differences in how we process information and emotions, we create environments and systems to help everyone thrive.

# Chapter 6 Left Brain And Right Brain Thinker

# Chapter 7

# Lack of a Blueprint

In a world brimming with established norms, career pathways, and social expectations, one might think that having a personal blueprint—a kind of roadmap for life—would be straightforward. But the reality is quite different. A significant number of us find ourselves navigating life without a clearly defined blueprint, which can create a sense of drifting or feeling lost. However, the absence of an initial blueprint does not mean a life sentence of aimlessness; rather, it opens up avenues for constructing our unique guide to life.

**How Blueprints Are Formed**

A life blueprint guides your path. It shows where you are headed and how to get there. Blueprints take shape from different parts of life. Your family teaches you things that shape it. School shapes it too. The people you know influence it as well. For some, a blueprint is laid out already. Their family or community plans things for them. This makes the path clear. But not everyone has this. And that is fine.

Think of building a house. You wouldn't just stack bricks and hope for the best. You need a plan first. That plan is the blueprint. It shows how to build the house you want. A house plan can change along the way. You might learn new things or need something different. Even without a plan at first, you can make one. Look at what has worked for others. Borrow their good ideas. Put your own spin on them.

Life blueprints come from many things. How you grew up matters. So does school. Social influences matter too. And your own experiences. Often a blueprint starts as rules from parents, teachers, or mentors. For some this works well. It guides them down a path that fits their talents and dreams. But for others, this handed-down blueprint does not fit right. It makes them uncomfortable, like clothes that don't suit them. For these people, a new blueprint is needed. One that reflects their true self.

The key is to build a life blueprint that fits you. Examine the parts that shape you - upbringing, education, social influences, and experiences. Take what works and leave what doesn't. Learn from others but make it your own. A good blueprint evolves over time. As you grow, it guides you down the path to becoming your best self. But it only works if it fits you well from the start. Take the time to create a life blueprint unique to who you are and who you want to become.

**Observing Others and Borrowing Ideas**

When you find yourself at a turning point in life without a clear path forward, looking at how other people have handled similar challenges can be very helpful. It's like being lost in an unfamiliar city. You could wander around aimlessly, or you could ask someone familiar with the area for directions. The people you observe become your living maps, giving you hints about different ways to reach your destination.

Watching others is not about copying them, like taking a photo of their lives and trying to recreate it. Instead, it's like learning the recipe for a dish you enjoyed at a restaurant, and then going home to make it your way with your favourite spices and cooking methods. By examining someone else's approach, you can gain new perspectives on solving problems, meeting challenges, or working toward goals.

For example, if you admire how someone built their career, try to understand the steps they took to get there. Did they start with small jobs and gradually move up? Did they invest in a lot of schooling or specialized training? Understanding these elements can give you a clearer idea of what might work for you. You can then adapt these insights to fit your life, integrating them into your own plan.

Similarly, if you see a friend who has a happy and healthy relationship with their family, you might wonder how they do it. Maybe they make spending quality time together a priority, or perhaps they communicate openly and honestly. Learning about these strategies doesn't mean you'll start living exactly like your friend. But it might inspire you to adopt some of the same habits, like setting aside time for family dinners or opening up more about your feelings.

The key to observing others and borrowing ideas is to be selective. Imagine your life as a unique painting that you're creating stroke by stroke. When you borrow ideas, you're adding new colours or techniques to make your painting even better. But remember, not every colour will fit into every painting, and the same goes for other people's life strategies. What works for one person might not work for you, and that's okay. The goal is to take what you think will improve your life, try it out, and see if it brings you closer to where you want to be.

Observing others and borrowing ideas is like shopping at a market filled with wisdom, experiences, and strategies. You don't need to buy everything you see. You can just pick what suits you and add it to your basket. Over time, you'll gather enough ingredients to create a life that's uniquely yours, using the best pieces of advice you've collected along the way.

**Piggybacking on Others**

Piggybacking is often seen in a negative light. People think it shows a lack of original ideas. However, when creating a personal roadmap for life, piggybacking can be very helpful. It lets you use proven plans and

## Chapter 7 Lack Of A Blueprint

strategies from others to build your own. Here is how it works and why it is so useful for making the life you want.

The main reason piggybacking works is because it speeds up learning. Someone else has already figured things out through trial and error. They have overcome obstacles, refined tactics, and achieved outcomes similar to your goals. By studying their success, you can learn important lessons without having to go through each struggle yourself. This is especially helpful in areas that need special skills or knowledge. It gives you a shortcut to capability.

Piggybacking is not about blindly copying someone. You need to think about the context behind their success. What worked for one person in a certain situation may not give you the same results. So it's crucial to understand the core principles that led to their achievements. The goal is to take the essence of their approach and adapt it to fit your unique needs, limits, and strengths.

Another benefit of piggybacking is reducing risk. Using a strategy that has already proven effective for someone else lowers the chance of catastrophic failure. This is very helpful in high-stakes areas of life like career moves or big lifestyle changes. Of course, it does not remove the risk entirely. But it can reduce the uncertainty considerably.

Piggybacking also lets you build on existing momentum. When you adopt a strategy already in motion, you harness the power of work already done. You do not have to start from scratch. You can hit the ground running and make faster progress. Of course, you still need to put in effort to see results. But standing on the shoulders of previous success gives you a head start.

At the same time, piggybacking requires humility. You must accept that someone else came up with effective solutions before you did. Ego can get in the way. But quelling the desire to reinvent the wheel clears the path for faster growth. Being open and humble enables learning.

Piggybacking also develops key analytical skills. You have to study various approaches objectively to discern their strengths and flaws. This builds critical thinking and judgment. It helps train your eye to identify the components that make a strategy succeed or fail. These analytical abilities can then be applied to other problems.

Piggybacking leverages the power of shared wisdom. It lets you benefit from the experience of those who have forged the path ahead. This does not make your journey effortless. But it can accelerate progress. With openness, insight and hard work, piggybacking provides a springboard to achieving your aims and aspirations.

Creating a life plan is like building a home. You get to decide the design. You choose which parts to build yourself and which to get from others. The end result is a structure unique to you.

When starting out, having examples to reference can help. Studying others' plans is useful. Builders often model new homes after existing designs that work well. But in the end, your home must fit you. It's the same with life plans.

Looking at how successful people and organizations do things can provide ideas. Their strategies can help you reach your goals faster. But you want to pick and choose carefully. Adopt only what aligns with your values, needs and objectives.

It's tempting to copy someone else completely. This saves effort. But it risks mismatch. Goals and values won't perfectly match. Dissatisfaction follows. Over-reliance on external models also reduces original thought. It hinders creative problem solving. So use others' strategies sparingly. See them as one of many tools for building your life.

Your life plan should be unique, like you. Think of yourself as a craftsman. Select useful bits and pieces from various sources. Integrate them into a structure tailored to you. This eclectic approach allows adaptability. It combines diverse views and tactics into a personalized whole.

## Chapter 7 Lack Of A Blueprint

For example, adopt your parent's work ethic. Blend it with a teacher's love of learning and a friend's emotional intelligence. Merge these to form your distinct life blueprint.

Building this plan takes investment. Deep self-reflection is needed to understand what's important to us. We need to adapt the useful parts for our goals and fill the gaps with new innovations.

The result is a solid foundation. Your unique life plan becomes a personal culture. This integrated set of beliefs, values, practices and objectives guides your choices. It becomes the measuring stick for opportunities. The lens for viewing challenges. The framework supporting your growth.

To conclude, the time spent crafting your plan pays off. Your life becomes more aligned with your true self. You follow a tailored blueprint allowing change and growth. This makes your path less stressful. More satisfying. It leaves room for life's unpredictable joys.

While having no pre-set course can seem challenging, it's an advantage. You get to build your life plan from the ground up. Pulling the best from varied sources creates something one-of-a-kind. Your personalized blueprint helps you live the life you want. It makes the journey as rewarding as the destination.

## Chapter 8

# Influences

In the intricate web of our existence, influences stand as the invisible threads that weave together the fabric of our thoughts, actions, and emotions. They can serve as guiding stars or misleading signals in the journey of life. Understanding the nature, origins, and impacts of these influences is pivotal for us striving to navigate the complexities of decision-making, interpersonal relationships, and self-discovery. This chapter aims to dissect the various layers of influences, examining their sources, manifestations, and effects on our thought processes.

**What are Influences?**

Influences are things that affect how we think, feel, and act. These can come from outside of us, like from the people we know or the culture we live in. Or they can come from inside of us, like our beliefs, past experiences, or even our genes. When these influences are obvious, we can clearly see how they shape who we are. For example, a mentor who guides your career is an influence you can plainly see. But often influences work quietly, slowly changing what we like, how we judge things, and how we think in ways we don't notice.

## Chapter 8 Influences

Influences from outside and inside of us work like mirrors and windows in our minds. As mirrors, they reflect back the values, ideas, and beliefs we've absorbed from the world around us. As windows, they give us new views to think about and use to form our own opinions, make choices, and pick up new habits. Influences are key both for reinforcing the ways we already think and for pushing our thinking in new directions.

Our friends and family are big outside influences that can mirror our own views back at us or open windows to new ideas. The place we live also presses its values and beliefs upon us in ways we often don't think about. Inside influences from our past experiences also mirror and bend our thoughts without us realizing it. The books we read, movies we watch, and news we take in are more outside influences that subtly shape the windows we see the world through. Even our genes can influence us from the inside out, shaping our personality and behaviour.

Of course, we also choose influences to shape our thinking. A student chooses to take a class to expand their knowledge. An employee reads books to pick up new skills. Or someone might join a new social group to be around different types of people. We can intentionally use influences as windows to grow even while other influences subconsciously mirror and shape our thoughts.

In a complex world filled with diverse cultures and viewpoints, understanding how influences work is key. We must recognize when our thinking is a mirror of limiting influences, whether from our upbringing, social circles, or biased news sources. And we need to keep opening windows by seeking out new ideas, experiences, and perspectives. This takes work. But becoming aware of the many influences shaping us is the first step toward gaining more control over our thoughts and beliefs.

### Where Do Influences Come From?

Influences that shape our lives come from many different places. Our family, friends, teachers, and co-workers all affect us. Even short interactions with people can change how we think, act, and feel. For example, how a parent punishes a child teaches them about authority. It shapes how they will interact with authority figures like teachers when they grow up.

The culture and society we live in is another big influence. Cultures have values, beliefs, and habits that affect everyone in the group. These unwritten rules set limits on how people should think and behave. They have a big impact on individuals and the whole community. Cultures help create national identities. They also decide what people should wear to events like weddings or funerals.

The media is a huge influence today. News sources shape people's political views. Social media affects how we see ourselves and what we think society expects of us. What we read, watch, or listen to gives us information. But it also frames how we see things. It can make us think and feel in certain ways.

Biology also plays a role. Our genes and brain chemistry can make us prone to act, feel, or think in certain patterns. For example, some people's genes make them react more strongly to stress. This can change how they make decisions and manage emotions.

By understanding where influences come from, we can spot what shapes our thoughts and actions. This awareness helps us take more control over our lives. We can make better choices and be mentally healthier when we know what affects us. Whether it's family, friends, culture, media, or biology, these influences surround us. Recognizing their impact is key to gaining more freedom over our decisions and well-being.

**How Are We Affected by Influences?**

Influences shape who we are in many ways. They affect how we act, think, and understand the world. For example, gestures like handshakes or bows show respect. We learn these from our culture. They become habits that we do without thinking. This shows how deep these influences can go.

Influences also shape our habits, both good and bad. Growing up in a home that values education might lead to the habit of studying hard. Hanging out with friends who use drugs could lead to unhealthy habits. Habits form when influences reinforce behaviours over time.

Influences also impact how we think and understand information. Our reasoning and problem-solving don't just come from within. They are shaped by our education, jobs, and social circles. Someone trained in science will tackle problems differently than someone trained in art. This demonstrates how influences shape our thought processes.

Influences seep into almost every part of our lives. They mold our actions, habits, and ways of thinking. We are who we are largely because of the many influences we absorb throughout our lives.

**Positive and Negative Influence Affects Our Thinking**

The ability to affect others is, in itself, neither good nor bad. Whether influence turns out to be positive or negative depends on the results it brings about. Good influences can help people grow, learn, and live better lives. A caring family, an inspiring teacher, or an experience that changes how we see the world can have a positive effect. They can shape our beliefs, give us confidence, and promote helpful behaviours. Positive influences often lead to better critical thinking, emotional intelligence, and understanding of how we interact.

On the other hand, bad influences can harm how we think and feel emotionally. Peer pressure, unhealthy relationships, and assumptions can lead to damaging behaviours and thoughts. Constant negative influences can make it harder to make good choices, see our true worth, and have a hopeful view of life. It is important to recognize these influences to lessen their impact and promote more positive thinking.

A supportive family can positively shape our worldview and instill confidence. An inspiring teacher can encourage constructive behaviours and lead to enhanced critical thinking skills. A transformative life experience can promote emotional intelligence and nuanced social understanding.

However, peer pressure can perpetuate harmful behaviours. Toxic relationships can reinforce destructive thought patterns. Societal stereotypes can skew our perception of self-worth. Constant negative influences can impair decision-making abilities and promote a cynical outlook on life.

It is crucial to identify positive and negative influences. Mitigate the impact of harmful pressures. Foster more constructive thinking by reducing exposure to negativity. Seek out supportive relationships that bring out your best qualities. Look for experiences that broaden your perspective. With care and intention, you can cultivate a mental landscape filled with positivity.

**What People Say Can Influence Our Thinking**

The words we use have power. What we say can plant seeds in someone's mind. Those seeds can grow into helpful thoughts or harmful beliefs. Kind words from people who care about us - like parents, teachers, or friends - can help us feel good about ourselves. Their words can give us courage to chase our dreams. But mean words or criticism, even if accidental, can hurt for a long time.

For example, a teacher who says, "You can do it!" may inspire a student to work hard and pursue a career. But a parent who says "You'll never make it" may destroy their child's confidence. The influence of others' words does not end in childhood. The conversations we have, the advice we listen to, and the remarks we overhear as adults all continue shaping our thoughts, solidifying our beliefs, and pushing us to take action for many years.

The words of people we admire often sway us the most. A respected mentor's encouragement may motivate us to step outside our comfort zone or view a situation in a new light. On the other hand, a careless comment from someone we admire can create self-doubt and second-

## Chapter 8 Influences

guessing. But we do not have to passively accept others' spoken opinions as fact. We can thoughtfully consider their words while staying true to our own inner voice.

Of course, the influence flows both ways. Our words have power too. What we say can uplift or disparage, inspire, or defeat. Our words can spark creativity in others or dim their inner light. Mindful, constructive communication requires self-awareness, empathy and care. Before speaking, we must consider both the literal meaning and implied message conveyed. With sensitive topics, a small dose of diplomacy helps ideas come across positively. And during conflict, respectful words focused on solutions rather than blame often yield the best outcome.

Ultimately, we choose whether to accept or reject others' spoken opinions of us and our potential. And we choose what messages our own words will carry. Of all the powers possessed by the human voice, the power to build others up or tear them down is among the greatest. We must use this power judiciously and responsibly. Our words can forge new paths of possibility or obstruct growth and progress. When people speak positively about their own abilities, it bolsters self-confidence. And when we offer encouragement rather than criticism, we help others see their own potential. With mindful communication, our words become seeds of hope and growth rather than seeds of harm.

### Brain Manipulation: The Dark Side of Influence

Manipulation happens when someone uses what they know about another person against them. They do this to get something for themselves, even if it hurts the other person. This ranges from subtle emotional pressure to very obvious mental tricks.

For example, a boss might pressure employees to work extra hours without pay. The boss could make the employees feel guilty if they say no. Or the boss might tell little lies to convince the employees they have to work overtime.

In personal relationships, manipulation often looks like emotional blackmail. We can use guilt or shame to get others to give us what we want.

These kinds of tricks often lead to unhealthy thinking. Our view of reality starts to change. Over time, we lose trust in ourselves and our own judgment. Our self-worth fades away, making it very hard to make good choices. It becomes difficult to see when others are manipulating us. This can cause serious emotional and psychological harm if we don't recognize it early on.

It is important to pay attention to how interactions with others make us feel. Do you feel worse about yourself or less sure of your own thoughts when you are with them? Do they often make odd requests and insist they are normal? Do they get very upset if you say no? These could be clues that the person is manipulating you.

If you suspect manipulation, try talking to a person you trust about the situation. They may be able to provide an outside perspective. You may want to reconsider the relationship if the manipulation continues. While ending a relationship can be very difficult, it may be necessary for your mental health.

Staying grounded in your own values can help combat manipulation. Remembering what is important to you and what you want out of life makes it easier to spot when someone pushes you off course. Having strong boundaries and being willing to say no are also key. You deserve respect. You do not have to go along with requests that make you uncomfortable, hurt you, or go against your values.

**Emotional Bullying as a Form of Negative Influence**

Bullying that attacks emotions can be just as harmful as physical bullying. While you can't see the damage emotional bullying causes, it still hurts. Emotional bullies try to control us by putting us down, embarrassing us, or spreading lies about us. When we are emotionally

## Chapter 8 Influences

bullied, we often would think badly about ourselves. We may feel worthless and lose confidence.

Being bullied in this way can seriously impact our mental health. It can make us stressed and anxious all the time. These feelings open the door for more negative thoughts that lead to bad choices. We might think that bullying is normal and okay as the bullying continues, and others make us feel worse and worse.

Influences are everywhere, coming from family, friends, culture, and strangers. These influences shape thoughts and actions. Positive influences help people grow. But negative influences can twist thinking and promote harmful behaviours.

It's important to understand these influences to know yourself and develop as a person. Taking in influence is not enough. You have to actively look at what affects your thoughts, beliefs and choices. Accepting that many things shape your life is the first step to taking control. Seeking positive influences and limiting negative ones allows us to build a better life.

In summary, emotional bullying damages in invisible ways. It causes stress, erodes self-worth and perpetuates harm. Influences, both good and bad, impact thinking and choices. Recognizing influence empowers growth. Limiting negative impact and increasing positive allows us to thrive.

## Chapter 9

# -Intrusive Thoughts - The Uninvited Mental Guests

Our minds are complex and mysterious. Sometimes thoughts pop into our heads that are troubling and seem to come out of nowhere. These kinds of thoughts are called intrusive thoughts. Intrusive thoughts can make people feel distressed, scared, or upset. Even though we might like to think we have complete control over our own minds, intrusive thoughts show that's not always true.

Intrusive thoughts are thoughts that seem to burst into our minds without us wanting them there. They arrive without invitation and overstay their welcome, leaving us puzzled and troubled. We did not consciously choose to think these thoughts, yet there they are inside our heads. Sometimes they are fleeting, but other times they stubbornly stick around against our wishes. We wonder, "Where did that thought come from?" and "Why can't I make it go away?"

These unwelcome mental intruders disrupt our peace of mind. When we are going about our daily lives, focusing on work, or connecting with

## Chapter 9 -Intrusive Thoughts -The Uninvited Mental Guests

loved ones, intrusive thoughts rudely barge in unannounced. They distract us and evoke unpleasant emotions like fear, disgust or doubt. We may feel ashamed of having such strange thoughts and try to push them out of awareness. However, suppressing intrusive thoughts often backfires by making them return stronger.

Though intrusive thoughts cause distress, they are a common and normal human experience. Most people have them at some point. They do not mean someone is flawed or crazy. However, when intrusive thoughts are very frequent or upsetting, professional help may be warranted.

**Where Do Intrusive Thoughts Come From?**

Understanding where intrusive thoughts come from is the first step to managing them. These thoughts barge in like rude guests, surprising you and messing up your mind. They come from many places - bad experiences like failing at something or getting your heart broken, hurtful words or criticism from others, or emotional and psychological scars from past traumas that still affect you. The random, sudden way these thoughts pop up can be especially upsetting. They interrupt your normal thinking, distract you, and can make you feel bad emotionally. So it's really important to understand where they come from, not just to satisfy curiosity but to actually help yourself cope with them. Their origins could be buried deep in your personal history, lying dormant for years before something happening now triggers them.

Intrusive thoughts are like weeds popping up out of nowhere in a garden you've tended with care. You need to figure out where they came from to properly pull them out by the roots. Did they grow from seeds blown in unpredictably by the wind, meaning they arose spontaneously with no clear cause? Or did they sprout from seeds laid long ago that now, under certain conditions, have decided to germinate?

In either case, learning the source of intrusive thoughts takes some gardening know-how and diligent inspection of the soil. Kneel down, dig around the base of the weed, and trace its roots as far down as you can go.

Examine the texture of the soil, notice rocks or hardened clay that may have blocked the roots from going deeper. Keep exploring gently but persistently, even if the roots twist out of sight.

Getting to the absolute bottom of the roots is often impossible. But uncovering even a portion of them can help you understand the conditions that allowed this weed to grow. Does the soil contain contaminants from past fertilizers that have destabilized the ecosystem? Is there a shallow layer of topsoil that encourages surface-level rooting? Are essential nutrients depleted in certain areas?

Your discoveries will inform the strategies you use to restore balance and order. Pulling the weed is just the first step. You'll also need to improve the soil, plant intentionally, and nourish the good seeds that will grow into a healthy garden. It's hard work, but the reward is a vibrant landscape you tend with care and joy.

The same is true in managing intrusive thoughts. Identifying where they came from, as best you can, gives you power over them. You realize the conditions that allowed them to take root, so you can start changing those conditions. It's a process - but like weeding a garden, the work you put in over seasons will make all the difference.

**Regrets, Mistakes, and Wrong Choices**

Making choices is a big part of our lives. Some of our choices don't matter much, like picking what to wear or eat. But other choices can change our lives forever. Having the freedom to choose for ourselves is great. But it also means we have to take responsibility for what happens after we choose. Nobody is perfect. We all make mistakes sometimes and choose wrong. Those mistakes can stay with us, making us feel bad long after they happen.

When our choices turn out bad, or we realize we chose wrong, it can really bother us. The memories of those mistakes keep popping back up in our heads. We can't stop thinking about what we did wrong, and how we wish we did things differently. These thoughts that keep coming back

# Chapter 9 - Intrusive Thoughts - The Uninvited Mental Guests

can make us feel down on ourselves. They can even make it hard to make more choices, because we're afraid we'll just mess up again. Stuck in the past, the mistakes make it tough to grow and feel good about ourselves now.

If we can step back and see those stuck thoughts for what they are - echoes of past mistakes, not signs we're bad people - it helps. Beating ourselves up over and over about a wrong choice we can't take back just makes us miserable. Those thoughts try to trick us into believing we're worthless because of some errors. But mistakes don't define anyone's true value or potential.

In our brains, those recurring thoughts about regrets are out of place, like weeds in a garden. They don't belong because they don't help us live our best lives in the present. We have to understand where the thoughts come from to pull them out by the roots. If we can connect them to the specific choices and times in our lives when we felt regret, it gets easier to handle them. Armed with that insight, we can start to take away their power over us.

Unwelcome thoughts are not random, they show up for a reason. Knowing that reason helps us address what's really bothering us instead of just feeling bad. Pulling up those mental weeds, and focusing our energy on growing new, positive thoughts is the best way forward. When we can push past the mistakes and see our true value, we take back control. Our minds become peaceful gardens again, where our self-esteem and potential can blossom.

**Bad Upbringing**

The way we grow up affects how we think and learn. Families shape children's emotional and thinking skills. From the time we're little to when we're teens, our home life builds our foundation. If kids don't get what they need, it can cause problems that last. Hurtful homes can lead to recurring thoughts that bother us. These thoughts echo the unstable places we grew up in. They follow us into adulthood and affect us in many ways.

For example, a child whose family only showed love when they behaved may struggle with thoughts about being worthy and lovable. Or a child who was often criticized or humiliated may battle self-doubt or extreme shyness as an adult. Because families are often the first social structure kids know, what we learn there sticks with us. It can be very hard to change. Seeing recurring thoughts as leftovers from a rocky childhood can help people identify why they struggle with thinking. This allows them to get the right psychological help.

The family environment shapes the way we see ourselves and the world. Warm, stable homes help children feel safe and valued. This gives them a solid base to build thinking skills. But hurtful, unstable homes have lasting effects. They undermine children's sense of security and self-worth. This leads to recurring negative thoughts that don't match reality. For instance, someone neglected as a child may struggle as an adult to see their worth. Even loving relationships may not ease their self-doubt.

There is a powerful tie between upbringing and cognitive health. Our thought patterns and coping strategies originate early in life. A child who couldn't depend on parents may become an anxious adult who expects rejection. An adult still haunted by childhood emotional abuse may battle low self-esteem. Even small daily stresses may echo old wounds.

The great news is that we can heal from our upbringing's effects with time and care. Counseling helps us understand where intrusive thoughts come from, building new social connections allows healthy relating skills to develop, and self-compassion helps counter old shame. There are many effective ways to rewrite old cognitive patterns.

While we can't change the past, we can change how we relate to it. Recognizing the root of intrusive thoughts helps decrease their power over us. They become understandable responses rather than unexplained burdens. This clarity guides us toward helpful solutions tailored to our unique life story. With care and courage, we can build new cognitive frameworks that support our health and dreams. Our upbringing shapes but does not define us. There is hope for all who seek it.

Chapter 9 -Intrusive Thoughts -The Uninvited Mental Guests

## Traumas and Abuse

Traumatic events can leave lasting marks on a our minds. These events can set the stage for intrusive thoughts that might continue for many years, possibly a whole lifetime. The sneaky nature of trauma-related intrusive thoughts is that they can pop up suddenly. They are set off by things that may seem unrelated or harmless. Trauma fundamentally changes how the brain handles information and responds to stress. It often makes the brain overly sensitive to triggers that can set off a rush of intrusive thoughts.

For example, someone who survived a car accident might experience intrusive thoughts when they hear the sound of screeching tires. Or someone who went through emotional abuse may feel overwhelmed by thoughts of not being good enough when faced with criticism. To make matters worse, the thoughts themselves can become triggers for more emotional and physical reactions. Like anxiety attacks. This creates a vicious cycle that is hard to break.

Healing from trauma takes time. The road is different for everyone. But with the right support, tools, and determination, we can learn to manage intrusive thoughts. The thoughts may never fully go away. However, their disruptive power can be greatly reduced. This makes room for more peace and presence in daily life.

## Innocence and Blaming Self

Intrusive thoughts are unwelcome ideas that seem to come from out of nowhere. They invade our minds when we least expect them. These troubling thoughts can make us feel ashamed, guilty, or afraid. Experts say intrusive thoughts are common. Most people have them at some point. But when intrusive thoughts happen a lot, they can really bother us.

Intrusive thoughts cause problems because they make us blame ourselves. Our minds can be very good at making us feel responsible, even for things that weren't our fault. Intrusive thoughts that come from misplaced blame are extra troubling. They create a false story about why the thought happened.

For example, someone bullied as a child might have intrusive thoughts that the abuse was their own fault. Their mind tells them they deserved it because of who they are. This distorted thinking can stick with them as a core belief. It colours how they see themselves in every situation after that. But the truth is they were innocent. The bullying was not their fault, no matter what their thoughts tell them. Realizing they are blaming themselves for no good reason is an important step. It helps them see the intrusive thoughts are lies, not truth.

Therapy focused on self-compassion can help. It teaches them not to believe the distorted ideas the intrusive thoughts create. Reminding themselves they did not deserve the bullying replaces false blame with true understanding.

Looking into what causes intrusive thoughts is useful too. A troubled childhood, trauma, or deep shame can all play a role. When we understand where intrusive thoughts come from, we can weaken their power over us. We can use therapy techniques targeted at their roots. This helps us handle intrusive thoughts in healthier ways.

The path to reclaiming peace of mind is not easy when intrusive thoughts have built false beliefs over time. But by facing their origins, we can unravel their hold on our emotional health. We can rewrite the false narratives they have created. With compassion, truth, and the right tools, we can find freedom from intrusive thoughts' harsh judgments. Our minds become calmer, clearer, and more focused on the present. We regain control of our thoughts and can live with self-acceptance.

The first step is recognizing that blame from intrusive thoughts is misplaced. This helps us take back power over our beliefs. Our thoughts can go from disturbing to quiet, from negative to neutral. In time we find clarity, perhaps for the first time in a long time. By easing suffering caused by intrusive thoughts, we ease our suffering as whole people. We end their unwarranted blame and change our relationship with ourselves.

**Dealing with Passive Thoughts, Planned Thoughts, and Active Thoughts**

## Chapter 9 - Intrusive Thoughts - The Uninvited Mental Guests

Our thoughts can be sorted into different groups based on how intentional they are and how much they impact what we do. Some thoughts just drift through our minds without having an immediate effect. These are passive thoughts. They might be as simple as remembering what you ate for breakfast or as complicated as thinking about the meaning of life in general. Other thoughts are on purpose and aimed at reaching specific goals. These planned thoughts are things like making a schedule for your day or figuring out a problem. Active thoughts lead directly to taking action right away. These thoughts guide our behaviour and choices we make.

The relationship between these kinds of thoughts and intrusive thoughts can be tricky. Passive thoughts can turn into intrusive thoughts when they are unwanted and get in the way. They sidetrack planned or active thoughts. For example, while getting ready to give a big presentation at work, intrusive thoughts about a recent breakup could break your focus and keep you from being as productive. Recognizing the type and nature of each thought can help people better control their thinking. Strategies that affect thinking can turn disruptive passive thoughts into planned or active thoughts that are helpful instead of harmful.

Rather than letting our minds wander wherever they want, it is helpful to take charge of our thoughts and guide them in productive directions. With practice, we can learn to minimize time spent on passive thoughts that have no purpose. We can also catch intrusive thoughts and turn our attention to more positive planned and active thoughts. This allows us to focus mental energy on achieving goals that are important to us.

A useful step is to become more aware of when our thoughts start to drift into passive or intrusive territory. Sometimes this happens without us even noticing at first. Checking in with ourselves regularly to monitor our thought patterns is important. When we tune into our thoughts, we can consciously decide how to respond to them. Rather than letting passive or intrusive thoughts take over, we can deliberately shift our focus.

We have power over our inner world of thoughts and don't have to let unhelpful thinking run wild. It simply takes commitment to exercise this mental muscle. With time, we can cultivate control over thoughts that once felt out of our control. Monitoring, evaluating and redirecting thoughts becomes easier. Progress won't happen overnight, but as we practice these skills our mental discipline will grow.

This process allows us to take an active role over our inner experience. We can move toward a place where our thoughts align with and support our goals and values. Rather than being controlled by passive and intrusive thoughts, we become equipped to intentionally craft thoughts that contribute to the life we want to build. Our thinking patterns can go from holding us back to propelling us forward.

**Negative Memory Cards Need to Be Replaced with Positive Ones**

People often remember bad experiences more clearly than good ones. This tendency has been linked to evolutionary psychology - our ancient survival instincts. Focusing on the negative helped early humans notice dangers and threats. But in the modern world, where most dangers are less immediate, this negativity bias can be harmful.

The bias shows up in intrusive thoughts as "negative memory cards." These are distressing thoughts that repeat in the mind, like a skipping record. They often recall past mistakes, regrets, failures - any kind of perceived shortcoming. To replace the negative cards, we need to purposefully acknowledge and appreciate positive experiences.

One way is practicing mindfulness. This means paying close attention to the present moment. When we feel joy or accomplish something, mindfulness helps us fully take it in. We can capture these little wins as they happen. Over time, they counterbalance the negative thoughts.

We can also look back purposefully for successes to celebrate. Remembering past achievements and wins helps build more positive memory cards. The more we actively seek out positives from our life, the more our brain retains them.

# Chapter 9 - Intrusive Thoughts - The Uninvited Mental Guests

Techniques like positive affirmations and gratitude journals are proven to rewire thinking. Affirmations are short phrases we repeat about our strengths and abilities. Saying them regularly combats negative self-talk. Gratitude journals help us regularly write down things we're thankful for. This builds up positive memories to draw on.

**Cancel the Past**

Dealing with the past can be tough. Sometimes the past just won't leave us alone. It keeps popping up in our thoughts and affecting what we do today. Those old memories and experiences are stored away in our minds like a big archive of files. When those files contain a lot of negative stuff, it weighs us down. It's like carrying around a heavy backpack everywhere you go. This extra weight makes it hard to think clearly and feel good.

So how can we "cancel the past" and feel freer emotionally and mentally? The first step is to open up those old memory files and take a fresh look. Are they still accurate? Are they still relevant to today? Getting help from a counselor or therapist can make this easier since old memories can be complex. They will work with you to reevaluate each past experience. Once you can see the past more clearly, its grip on the present will loosen.

Intrusive thoughts that pop up unwanted are also tangled up in our past experiences. These disruptive thoughts have roots in many places - our personal history, the way our brains work, the biases we've developed over time. To reduce intrusive thoughts, we need to trace back to the source and understand what's causing them. Helpful tools include therapy techniques, mindfulness practices, and purposefully changing our thought patterns. This takes effort but can make a big difference in reclaiming mental space.

In conclusion, the past does not have to define us. We can decrease its influence in the here and now. This takes courage to confront old memories, guidance to reassess them, and commitment to let them go. Though challenging, this work can free up our minds, improve emotional health, and allow us to live more fully in the present. With help and perseverance, we can break the grip of the past. We can refuse to allow old hurts or habits to weigh us down. Step by step, we can create space for clearer thinking and greater inner peace.

# Chapter 9 - Intrusive Thoughts - The Uninvited Mental Guests

Chapter 10

# The Intricacies of Positive and Negative Thought Patterns

Our minds are complex. Thoughts constantly appear like stars lighting up a night sky. Some thoughts shine brightly with hope and positivity. Others seem dimmed by negativity and fear. What causes this difference between positive and negative thinking? The answer lies in understanding the brain's biology and evolution. This chapter offers an in-depth look at the mechanics behind how our brains produce thoughts.

**How Does the Brain Produce These Thoughts?**

In the brain, nerve cells called neurons generate thoughts. When neurons fire in certain patterns, thoughts emerge in our mind. Chemical messengers called neurotransmitters act like conductors of an orchestra. They regulate the emotional quality of thoughts. For example, the neurotransmitter serotonin promotes feelings of happiness and well-being. This can lead to more positive thinking. Another neurotransmitter,

## Chapter 10 The Intricacies Of Positive And Negative Thought Patterns

dopamine, is tied to pleasure and reward. It sparks thoughts that motivate actions. An imbalance in these neurotransmitters may tip thinking toward the negative.

But what triggers neurons to fire in the first place? The brain's plasticity allows it to adapt and change. The neural circuits behind thoughts are dynamic, not fixed. External experiences can activate these circuits, shaping thinking. Sensory input, social interactions, even internal body states can influence neuronal firing. The brain's reward and punishment systems also play a role. Positive experiences that align with our goals may switch on circuits linked to upbeat thoughts. Negative experiences may activate circuits associated with pessimistic thinking.

Life experiences shape and prune these connections through neuroplasticity. A child constantly exposed to words develops language circuits. Learning to play an instrument build new musical pathways. Trauma can forge hypervigilant threat detection channels. But the brain's lifelong adaptability means neural wiring remains open to change. With care and effort, even rigid thought patterns can be remapped.

By unveiling the hidden workings of the brain, science illuminates the root of human thinking. While thoughts may seem ephemeral and insubstantial, they arise from tangible electrical signals and chemical messengers within the brain's vast neural network. Understanding these foundational mechanisms allows us to nurture positive thinking and weed out negative thought patterns at their source. The brain's malleable circuits mean our thoughts need not remain fixed but can be reshaped through conscious effort. By harnessing the brain's plasticity, we gain the power to transform our inner world.

**The Neurological Reasoning**

The brain is an incredibly complex organ made up of many different parts that all work together. Each part has its own specific job. Understanding how these different parts connect and communicate is key to learning how our thoughts are formed.

One important area of the brain involved in creating thoughts and emotions is called the limbic system. The limbic system includes structures like the amygdala, hippocampus, and hypothalamus. This system plays a big role in making emotions and emotional thoughts.

For example, the amygdala is often called the "emotional center" of the brain. When we have an intense emotional experience, especially one involving fear or stress, the amygdala springs into action. When activated, the amygdala makes the brain more tuned in to negative thoughts.

However, the limbic system is not the only player. Another important part called the prefrontal cortex is critical too. The prefrontal cortex handles higher level thinking abilities like planning, decision-making, and controlling social behaviour. It can balance out emotional signals coming from the limbic system. With its reasoning powers, the prefrontal cortex can generate more positive, rational thoughts. But it needs helpful input from other areas to do this well.

The complex interactions between the limbic system, prefrontal cortex, and other regions let us regulate our emotions. This process allows us to find a balance between emotional and logical thinking.

Understanding these neurological links makes clear that thoughts don't just happen randomly. They are created through finely tuned pathways in the brain. Learning about these pathways also sheds light on how therapies can "rewire" the circuits in our brains. This makes it possible to shift thinking from negative to positive.

**Why Does the Brain Produce Thoughts to Protect Itself?**

The main job of the brain goes far past just thinking clearly. It is the control center that is responsible for keeping us alive. From an evolutionary perspective, thoughts - whether positive or negative - play a defensive role. The brain interprets the information from our senses, compares it to past experiences and knowledge, and then creates thoughts as adaptive responses.

Chapter 10 The Intricacies Of Positive And Negative Thought Patterns

Negative thoughts can act like internal alarm systems. For example, feeling afraid after hearing an unexpected noise in a dark alley can trigger the "fight or flight" response. This prepares our bodies to face potential danger. Neurotransmitters and hormones like adrenaline and cortisol are released. These sharpen focus, increase alertness, and get the muscles ready for quick action. Negative thoughts are not inherently "bad." In certain situations, they can be life-saving.

Similarly, positive thoughts have evolved to strengthen behaviours that are beneficial for survival. The joy felt while eating, for instance, makes sure that people look for nourishment, which is essential for survival. This pleasure feeling is created by the release of dopamine. This encourages us to repeat this beneficial action in the future. In social interactions, positive thoughts improve cooperation, strengthen social bonds, and generally promote behaviours that are good for community living. This was an evolutionary advantage for us.

**The Balancing Act of Positive and Negative Thoughts**

Our thoughts shape our reality. Both positive and negative thinking play key roles in our mental health. Finding balance between them is critical, but not always easy.

Life brings many stressors that can push our thoughts in a more negative direction. Trauma, isolation, or constant anxiety tilt the scales, making us prone to more pessimism. This is when negative thinking can become problematic, especially if it lasts a long time or feels too intense to manage.

The brain reacts strongly to chronic stress. Stress hormones like cortisol alter brain structure and function when elevated for too long. Regions like the hippocampus, vital for memory and emotion, are impacted. This brain change makes negative thinking more likely, setting up a vicious cycle.

Positive experiences provide an antidote to negative thought patterns. Activities that evoke "feel good" neurotransmitters like serotonin and endorphins restore balance. Mindfulness, gratitude practices, and focusing on positives train the brain away from negativity.

The good news is our brains remain flexible throughout life. Neural pathways that reinforce negative thinking can be rewired. New healthy circuits for interpreting experiences can be built.

By recognizing and challenging negative thoughts, new mental frameworks emerge. Repeated practice of these cognitive exercises establishes fresh neural patterns, weakening old negative ruts.

Medications like antidepressants also target biological roots of negative thinking. They aim to increase serotonin availability in the brain, thereby promoting positivity. However, a personalized approach is best, considering each person's unique factors.

In conclusion, our thoughts arise from a blend of nature and nurture. While negative thinking can serve survival needs, too much becomes harmful. Environmental stressors play a role, but so does our neurobiology. The key is finding the balance between positive and negative.

Thankfully, the brain stays changeable. We can influence our thinking by how we care for both mind and body. Simple practices build up positive neural circuits. Therapy and medication also adjust underlying biology. Though it takes work, we can guide our thoughts toward health and hope.

The intricacies of our minds remain profound. But by understanding the interplay between brain function, life experience, and thought patterns, we gain power over our inner world. Small steps daily toward more positive thinking compound over time, bringing the light of optimism back into focus. The journey requires patience, but we all have potential for progress.

# Chapter 10 The Intricacies Of Positive And Negative Thought Patterns

Chapter 11

# The Blueprint for Thought Mastery

Welcome to an important chapter that will serve as both a guide and a mirror. The goal here is to explore what it means to champion our thoughts. We will look at the mindset that defines champions across various fields. Much like an athlete train to be the best in sports, we can use similar strategies to master our own thoughts. This chapter invites you to not just control or manage your thoughts, but to actually transform them into tools for achieving your life goals.

**Who is a Champion? Think Like an Athlete.**

The classic image of a champion is often someone standing on a podium, bathed in the glow of victory. While this captures a moment of triumph, it does not show the years of hard work, setbacks, and personal growth that led to that win. A champion is not just a title earned through a single achievement. It is an identity built through ongoing discipline, resilience, and relentless pursuit of excellence.

## Chapter 11 The Blueprint For Thought Mastery

Athletes are a great example for understanding this. Elite athletes have characteristics that allow them to excel. Their success is not just physical ability. Their mental conditioning is equally important. Their minds are trained to focus, adapt, and overcome. This mental training, though often overlooked, is the backbone of their success. Thinking like an athlete goes beyond sports. It means adopting a disciplined, focused, and resilient mindset aimed at continuous improvement in any chosen field, including the ongoing task of shaping one's thoughts.

To be a champion, you must put in the work. Success does not happen overnight. It takes years of practice, failures and getting back up again. Athletes spend hours each day perfecting their craft. They have a growth mindset, believing their abilities can be developed through dedication and persistence. Developing champion thoughts requires the same commitment. It takes regular practice through techniques like meditation or journaling. And it requires the resilience to keep trying when you stumble.

Champions are focused and intentional. They zero in on their goals with laser-like precision. Distractions and self-doubt do not deter them. Cultivating our best thoughts requires similar mental conditioning. It means focusing our minds completely on the present moment, not drifting to regrets about the past or worries about the future. It means screening out negative self-talk and zeroing in on uplifting truths. Developing intense mental focus takes work but pays dividends.

Champions are adaptable and open to coaching. When setbacks happen, they analyze what went wrong and adjust their strategies. They consult mentors and experts to gain new insights. Managing our thoughts also requires flexibility. When specific thought patterns prove unhelpful, we must be willing to try new ways of thinking. Feedback from others can reveal blind spots. The path to mental mastery includes an openness to change course.

**Comparing a Champion with Championing Our Thoughts**

Becoming an expert at a skill or sport and becoming an expert at managing our thoughts have a lot in common. Just like a champion must get past external barriers to become very good at what they do, becoming an expert at managing our thoughts means overcoming internal barriers, many of which we create ourselves. Both take a strict set of traits like discipline, resilience, and a commitment to always improving.

For example, an athlete puts in countless hours of practice, sticks to a strict diet, and is evaluated in ways that go beyond just their sport. The athlete knows that every part of their life affects how they play. Similarly, becoming an expert at managing our thoughts requires a comprehensive approach. It's not just about avoiding negative thoughts but also actively creating a positive mindset. We must train our minds with as much dedication as an athlete trains their body and skills.

It's important to recognize that becoming a champion in any area involves having a lifestyle fully focused on that goal. The same is true for our thoughts. We can't expect to have a healthy mental state while ignoring key things like emotional well-being, physical health, or relationships. The act of becoming an expert at managing our thoughts is, therefore, a commitment to fully improving ourselves. It requires the kind of comprehensive approach that athletes use to excel in their sports, focusing not just on the sport itself but on everything that contributes to their performance. It's not just about having the right thoughts but about creating an environment where those thoughts can grow.

**The Purpose of Championing Our Thoughts**

Mastering our thoughts is an important goal. It goes beyond just organizing our minds or making ourselves feel better. The real purpose is to create big changes in our inner world that lead to big changes in our outer lives. It's about taking charge of our personal growth and well-being. Thoughts drive actions, feelings, and the direction we take in life. An athlete pushes their physical limits to achieve great feats. Mastering our thoughts unlocks deeper mental and emotional abilities.

This purpose matters because thoughts are central to being human. They shape emotions, guide choices, and set life's path of goals and relationships. Mastering our thoughts lays a strong foundation for building our lives. Like athletes strengthen their body, the mind is a sacred place to care for and develop. Athletes exercise their muscles to excel physically. Mastering thoughts exercises our mental abilities to excel in difficult life situations. This gives us more control and improves decision-making, relationships, resilience, and achieving our aims.

There are two key benefits. First, it empowers us to shape our life's story instead of letting outside forces write the script. Second, it helps us connect better with the world. A well-cared-for mind is better at meaningful relationships, opportunities, and contributing to society. An athlete inspires by achieving great feats. Mastering our thoughts inspires others through the wisdom and poise we gain.

Seeing the full impact highlights the importance of commitment. It's not just avoiding negative thoughts or being positive sometimes. It's an ongoing effort to create an enriched mental environment where our best qualities thrive. This purpose is the foundation for what follows. Each part offers guidance on how to achieve mastery of our thoughts. Keeping this vision in mind makes the commitment more meaningful.

## Characteristics and Traits of a Champion and Their Thoughts

Mastering our thoughts requires dedicated effort over time. Like a champion athlete or business leader, we must nurture certain qualities if we want to succeed. By studying how champions achieve success, we can learn valuable lessons to apply to managing our thinking.

First, we need discipline. Champions stick to rigorous training routines and careful diets. They don't skip workouts or eat junk food. When it comes to our thoughts, discipline means staying mentally tough. Resist negative thinking and distractions. Instead, focus on goals and positive ideas. We need to build the habit of steering our minds toward constructive places, not letting it wander aimlessly.

Second, focus intently on one thing at a time. Champions block out everything around them and zero in on the task at hand. Similarly, we should concentrate fully on positive thoughts, tuning out anything that clutters our minds or drags us down. Minimize mental distractions so we can channel our brainpower purposefully.

Third, bounce back from setbacks. Champions inevitably face failures and defeats on their way to the top. What sets them apart is they learn from losses and come back stronger. The same goes for our thinking. When we slip into negativity or stress gets the best of us, reflect on what went wrong. Then develop strategies to better manage our thoughts next time. Resilience is key.

Fourth, feel passionate about improving your mental health. Champions derive fuel from their deep love of their sport or business. Half-hearted interest won't cut it. We need genuine excitement to drive our efforts and sustain commitment. View mastering your thoughts not as a chore but a goal you feel motivated to keep pursuing.

Fifth, know yourself, flaws and all. Champions recognize their weaknesses as well as strengths. You need the same self-awareness about your thought patterns. Identify triggers that lead to negative thinking. Understand where your mental resilience needs work. The more familiar you are with your own mind, the better you can shape your thinking.

Sixth, keep adapting your strategies. Champions know that standing still means falling behind. They alter their game plans as needed, adjusting to new challenges. As you work to improve your thinking, be open to changing tactics. Refine your coping methods or try different mindfulness techniques as you gain insight into your thought habits. An adaptable approach is key.

Seventh, envision the big-picture goals driving your daily progress. Champions set long-term objectives that guide their short-term actions. Get clear on your overarching mental health goals too, whether achieving lasting happiness, building emotional resilience or adopting a more

## Chapter 11 The Blueprint For Thought Mastery

positive mindset. Let your vision direct your daily thought management efforts.

Finally, stay humble. Champions acknowledge the role of mentors, teammates and luck in their success. They know they don't have all the answers. Likewise, admit you don't have everything figured out when it comes to managing your mind. Be open to learning, whatever your experience level. Recognize that mastering your thoughts is an ongoing journey.

By recognizing and nurturing these traits, we can lay a strong foundation for becoming champions of our thoughts. Much like an athlete who utilizes these characteristics to achieve physical mastery, individuals can adopt these traits to cultivate a mental environment conducive to well-being, resilience, and overall life satisfaction. The end goal is not just to manage or control thoughts but to actually transform them into powerful allies on the path to fulfilling life goals.

Thinking like a champion is about having a positive yet realistic mindset. It means being optimistic but also acknowledging challenges and being ready to take them on. Champions are always prepared. They make plans and adapt when needed. They combine a sunny outlook with hard work to reach their goals.

This winning mindset is not something you are just born with. It is learned over time through practice, experience, and self-reflection. For example, athletes use physical and mental training to improve. They look for any advantage they can get - not just in their bodies but in their minds too. This helps them stay tough when things get hard. By doing this, they show that preparation plus opportunity often leads to what we call luck.

Similarly, having the mindset of a champion involves more than wishful thinking. It means taking real steps toward clearly defined goals to back up your positive thoughts.

Champions also never stop improving. They do not just rest after a win. They look for ways to keep getting better, setting goals to top their personal bests. This connects closely to having a "growth mindset". This means believing your abilities can grow through hard work, good strategies and input from others. Those with this mindset thrive on challenges. They see them as chances to learn, not obstacles. This makes it a key part of thinking like a champion.

The champion's mindset combines optimism, preparation, adaptation, goal-setting and constant improvement. It is not about ignoring or glossing over problems. It is about tackling them head-on with a constructive attitude. Champions make detailed plans yet stay flexible. They balance positive thinking with diligent effort. Their self-belief comes from proven progress, not just motivational mantras. This learned mentality helps elite athletes, business leaders and others reach ever-higher levels of achievement. It takes work to develop, but the rewards make it worth the effort.

**Train Your Thoughts Like a Champion**

Thinking like a champion is just the first step. The next step is training our thoughts to match this mindset. This involves looking inward and actively practicing new ways of thinking. Athletes undergo tough training routines. These not only build physical strength but also improve mental toughness, focus, and strategic thinking. Similarly, training our thoughts takes a systematic and disciplined approach.

Cognitive restructuring is one method to train our thoughts. It means catching yourself when you have negative or harmful thought patterns. Then analyze these thoughts to understand where they come from. After that, consciously replace them with more constructive or realistic beliefs. This practice aims to shift ingrained thinking habits. It steers thoughts toward more positive and productive directions. This strategy is like an athlete studying video of their flawed technique. Then they follow up by practicing the right method until it becomes natural.

Another powerful tool for training the mind is mindfulness meditation. This involves staying present and fully engaged in the here and now. Studies show mindfulness can greatly reduce mind-wandering. Especially the kind of mind-wandering linked to destructive or negative thoughts. Practicing mindfulness can bring mental clarity. This allows you to examine your thoughts and make more reasoned choices.

Then there is the role of tracking progress. This is like how athletes measure performance gains through various metrics. Keeping a journal of thought patterns, emotions, and actions can provide valuable insights. It can help identify triggers for negative thinking. And it shows how these thoughts lead to actions. This data can further refine and improve thought training methods.

Like athletes break down long-term goals into smaller, achievable objectives, we should aim for measurable milestones in thought training. This makes the whole process less intimidating and more manageable. It offers regular opportunities for small victories that can significantly boost motivation.

In conclusion, championing our thoughts integrates resilience, strategic optimism, and constant improvement into personal thinking. Like a well-trained athlete, this requires dedication, self-reflection, and consistent efforts to challenge and expand mental boundaries. Mastering one's thought processes not only improves personal well-being. It also has far-reaching benefits for professional and personal relationships, enhancing overall quality of life.

## Chapter 12

# I Am Not My Thoughts

As we navigate the intricate corridors of life, we're continually guided and, at times, misled by our thoughts. Our experiences, aspirations, fears, and judgements, creates a backdrop against which we interpret the world and ourselves. While our thoughts serve as valuable guides, providing insight and prompting action, they can also become oppressive dictators, swaying our moods, and dictating our behaviour. This chapter aims to dismantle the often-conflated relationship between our thoughts and our true selves. By dissecting the complexities of our thinking, mental health, stress, and self-blame, it seeks to emancipate others from the tyranny of their own mind.

**Everyone Has Negative and Positive Thoughts**

We all have both positive and negative thoughts. This is normal, not a flaw. Having different kinds of thoughts helps us survive and do well. Positive thoughts reward us when we do good things. They make us want to help others and better ourselves. Negative thoughts warn us of danger. They make us cautious and careful.

## Chapter 12 I Am Not My Thoughts

But too many negative thoughts can be a problem. In our society, people often see negative thoughts as bad and try to avoid them. However, we need both positive and negative thoughts to understand the world fully.

Without negative thoughts, we might take dangerous risks. We need those worries to be careful. But without positive thoughts, we would have no drive to improve. Our hopes push us forward.

Life changes how we feel. Hard times can make us dwell on the negative. Good times bring more positive thinking. The types of thoughts we have change, but everyone has both kinds.

What matters most is how we react to our thoughts. Do we listen to warnings and avoid harm? Do we believe in ourselves enough to keep trying? How we manage all our thoughts, good and bad, shapes who we are.

Knowing everyone has ups and downs can help us. It means no one escapes negative thoughts, even happy people. And even gloomy people find joy sometimes. We all have both kinds of thoughts, just in different amounts.

This mix of thoughts makes us human. We all share it, and it connects us. The range of thinking, from dark to light, is part of everyone's mind. We each build our mental world from the same tools - the thoughts we're given.

With care and wisdom, we can use our mix of feelings to grow. We can embrace the positive while heeding the negative. Our shared inner landscape offers chances to find our own path between its peaks and valleys.

### Mental Health and Its Relation to Negative Thoughts

Mental health and negative thinking have a complicated relationship. For many people, mental health problems like depression, anxiety, and obsessive-compulsive disorder are breeding grounds for negative thoughts. The chemical imbalances in the brain that come with these conditions often distort thinking, making it very hard to break free from constant negativity. At the same time, negative thoughts themselves can make mental health worse and cause symptoms or even the start of these conditions. It's a two-way street: mental health affects thoughts, and thoughts affect mental health.

But how does this happen exactly? Brain chemicals like serotonin, dopamine, and norepinephrine have a big impact on mood and thought patterns. Abnormal levels of these chemicals can lead to distorted or overly negative ways of thinking. These chemicals interact with the brain's circuitry, influencing how information is processed and decisions are made. For example, someone with depression may focus more on noticing, remembering, and thinking about negative events rather than neutral or positive ones. This skewed attention and memory further reinforces negative thoughts, creating a cycle that is hard to break without professional help.

However, it's important to also consider environmental factors and life experiences that could contribute to negative thoughts and poor mental health. Traumatic experiences, discrimination, or long periods of extreme stress can make the brain prone to our thinking negatively and worsen our mental health conditions. Therefore, fully understanding the relationship between mental health and thoughts requires looking at both biological and environmental factors.

The interaction between mental health and negative thinking is complicated, involving chemical imbalances, brain pathways, environmental triggers, and personal experiences. They mutually influence each other, contributing to a cycle that can either spiral downward or be redirected toward our improvement. Understanding this relationship is essential for us wanting to achieve better mental health and more balanced thinking.

### Stress and Its Relation to Negative Thoughts

Managing stress is key to mental health. When we feel threatened, our brains react in an evolutionary way to protect us. However, this reaction can often cause more harm than good in the modern world.

## Chapter 12 I Am Not My Thoughts

When the brain senses danger, whether the threat is real or just perceived, it sounds an alarm. This alarm activates our body's stress response. Part of this response is the release of cortisol, known as the "stress hormone." Cortisol primes the body to take immediate action. This reaction helps us react quickly to survive immediate physical threats. However, in today's world, we activate this response frequently in response to emotional threats too. Our stress response can't tell the difference between a tiger attack and a worrying thought. Our bodies end up in emergency mode way too often.

Frequent stress responses impair our thinking skills. High cortisol levels make it hard to think rationally, plan ahead, and stay positive. Instead, the brain looks for potential threats everywhere. It generates constant worries, fears, and repetitive thoughts. The original stressor leads to more and more anxious thinking. This locks us into an unhealthy cycle.

Understanding how stress biologically impacts thinking is powerful. It means we can break the cycle with both physical and mental tools. For example, exercise reduces cortisol. Meditation builds skills to detach from anxious thoughts. Medications also help, especially for severe cases.

We also have to look at root causes of stress in our lives. Finances, work, discrimination, and family issues often trigger stress responses. Dealing with these social factors brings long-term relief. A holistic approach includes all parts of life, not just symptoms.

Stress is guaranteed in life. But we can change how it affects thinking. Using a range of biological, mental, and social solutions, we can break the link between stress and negative thoughts. This frees us up to live healthier lives, using our minds in more positive ways. With knowledge and skills, we can rewrite the script stress writes in our brains. We can replace it with one that enhances our lives rather than impairs them. Even severe cases can be improved with persistence.

In essence, how we think under stress is flexible, not fixed. By managing stress holistically, from all angles, we can retrain our minds for health. We can reduce the evolutionary reactions that worked for survival but now cause mental harm. With practice, we can transform stress from an enemy into just another part of life, one that no longer controls our thoughts and lives.

**I Am Not to Blame for My Negative Thoughts**

Blame can sneak into our minds and cause problems. It makes us feel guilty or ashamed about our thoughts. Many people think they are responsible for their negative thoughts. This adds more distress to thoughts that are already upsetting. But as we've learned, negative thoughts often just pop up on their own. They are automatic. Many things can trigger them - our biology, past experiences, or stress. Understanding this can take away the blame. If we are kind to ourselves, we see that negative thoughts aren't because we are flawed or bad. They are a normal human experience. In the same way you wouldn't blame yourself for catching a cold, blame doesn't make sense for automatic negative thoughts.

Our minds can play tricks on us. Thoughts can turn against us before we even notice. But we don't have to believe everything our minds tell us. Just because a thought pops up doesn't mean it's true or that we wanted it there. We all have unhealthy thoughts sometimes. It's easy to start questioning ourselves when they show up. Are we bad people for thinking this? Do these thoughts reveal some darkness inside us? In reality, random negative thoughts don't define who we are. They are just stray signals crossing our minds. We can acknowledge them and let them pass without judgment.

Beating ourselves up over our thoughts creates needless suffering. Blame and guilt stir up awful feelings on top of the original upset. This extra layer of distress can make an already difficult situation feel unbearable. The truth is our thoughts don't always represent our true feelings and values. Negative thoughts can contradict what we stand for. Judging ourselves for them is inaccurate and unhelpful. With self-acceptance, we can create space between ourselves and unwanted thoughts. We recognize they don't represent who we really are.

## Chapter 12 I Am Not My Thoughts

In many ways, thoughts have a mind of their own. They arise automatically from our brains' circuitry. Our past experiences wire our brains to react in certain ways without our control. For example, if someone criticizes us, circuits may light up that make us feel worthless. This doesn't mean we are worthless. It's just our brains falling into old reaction patterns. We can rewire these patterns over time. But in the moment, unkind thoughts are just thoughts, not facts. We don't have to own them or beat ourselves up over them. They came from our brains' conditioning, not our true selves.

Blame and guilt keep us stuck in pain. They prevent us from moving forward in a healthy way. Self-compassion opens the door to growth and healing. When we stop judging ourselves for our thoughts, we can see them clearly for what they are - automatic reactions, not who we are. We can accept ourselves with all our quirks and wiring. From this place of self-kindness, we gain the strength to care for ourselves and retrain our minds in healthier directions. The path forward starts with self-acceptance, not self-blame. Our thoughts don't define us, but how we respond to them does. We can choose understanding over judgment and start building lives of meaning, even with the noisy minds we've been given.

**I Cannot Blame Others for My Negative Thoughts**

Each of us has likely blamed others for the negative thoughts in our heads. It's easy to point fingers at the people and events around us. We say our difficult childhood or bad relationships caused unhealthy thinking. We claim society and peer pressure created our issues. But even if life has dealt you a tough hand, you still have power over your mindset.

External factors don't fully control how we process life. We can choose whether to let circumstances shape our thoughts and actions. By taking responsibility for our reactions, we reclaim our personal agency. Even when negative thinking is forced on us, the power to manage those thoughts rests within us.

Past hardships or toxic people can influence how we see the world. But we get to decide what meaning to assign those experiences. We can let them make us bitter and broken. Or we can use them to grow stronger and wiser. Our interpretation of events - not the events themselves - fuels our perspective.

Stress and mental health struggles also impact thinking patterns. When anxiety or depression sets in, negative thoughts often follow. But a mental health condition does not define us completely. It does not tell the whole story of who we are or what we're capable of. We are far more complex than any diagnosis could capture.

In the same way, passing thoughts - positive or negative - do not reflect our full value. We are multifaceted beings with diverse qualities and potential. We should not judge our worth based only on our cognition. We should not let a few dark mind loops convince us that we are flawed or unworthy.

Life experience molds our perspective but does not cement it. With self-awareness, we can challenge unhelpful thought patterns. We can rewrite the meaning we assign challenging circumstances and tap into our inner wisdom and strength.

To conclude, by taking a balanced view of the relationship between the self and thought, we gain freedom. We need to recognize that we are more than our negative rumination and self-criticism. We are more than our stressors and diagnoses. We have the power to manage our inner world amid outer chaos. We can override patterns that no longer serve us and become the author of our inner narrative.

# Chapter 12 I Am Not My Thoughts

## Chapter 13

# Break Self-Destructive Thoughts

This chapter looks at harmful thinking patterns that can trap us and leave us stuck with dark thoughts. It is important to understand this issue because these thoughts impact more than just moods. They influence actions, relationships, and overall wellness. This chapter will identify harmful thought patterns, look closely at behaviours that continue them, and give useful strategies to break free. Whether the thoughts show up as constant self-pity, self-centeredness, or acting out for attention, recognizing them is the first move toward reclaiming mental freedom.

**What Carry Self-Destructive Thoughts**

Unhelpful thinking patterns can steer us in the wrong direction. These thoughts make us do things, decide things, or feel things that are not good for us. They might pop up now and then or be deep habits that colour how we see the world and ourselves. These thoughts come in many forms - doubting ourselves, feeling defeated, or expecting the worst, to name a few. Each one can negatively impact different parts of our lives, from self-esteem to relationships and careers.

The sneaky thing about these thoughts is how they feed themselves. For example, the thought "I'm not good enough" could stop you from applying for a job. Then you end up unemployed, which seems to prove the original thought right.

It's important to understand unhelpful thoughts because they often open the door to harmful actions and consequences. They act like distorted lenses that make everything seem to confirm their misleading story. To break this cycle, we first need to identify these thoughts for what they are: distortions, not truths. Once we spot them, we're in a better place to challenge and counteract them. We can use strategies like reframing our thinking or mindfulness to reshape our thought patterns in a more constructive way.

These distorted thoughts can sneak up on us. Left unchecked, they cause us to view ourselves and the world through a negative, hopeless lens. We see failure as certain and progress as impossible. In this mindset, we are prone to act in self-limiting or even self-destructive ways that align with the harmful stories we tell ourselves.

The first step is noticing when these thought patterns arise. Instead of automatically believing them, ask yourself: Is this thought helpful? Is it absolutely true? Or is it a distortion? What would be a more balanced, truthful viewpoint?

Once you identify the twisted thinking at play, you can start untwisting it. For example, replace broad labels like "I'm a failure" with specifics like "I failed at this particular task." Notice catastrophizing thoughts and replace them with calmer, more measured perspectives.

With practice, we can catch and reshape unhelpful thoughts before they send us down the wrong path. The more we challenge our distorted narratives, the less power they have over us. We can reclaim a clear-eyed view of ourselves and the world, acting with self-compassion instead of self-destruction.

**Avoid Feeling Sorry for Yourself**

Feeling constant self-pity keeps us stuck in negative thinking. While self-pity may temporarily make us feel better, it usually keeps us focused on the bad things. Over time, always thinking about our problems make us feel like a victim. We start to blame other people or things for our troubles and forget that we can take action. This makes a loop where not taking action leads to no progress, which confirms our thought that life is against us.

To break out of this harmful mindset, we need to challenge the urge to feel sorry for ourselves. We can do this by looking at the facts for and against our thoughts, identifying exaggerated thinking, and shifting our focus to solving problems. As we change from a victim mentality to a problem-solving view, we empower ourselves and undermine the basis of self-destructive thoughts.

Breaking free of self-destructive thoughts is about changing our life path, improving our mental health, and reaching our full potential. This chapter is a guide to help us identify, face, and dismantle these harmful thought patterns. This allows us to steer our lives in a more positive and fulfilling way.

**Avoid Narcissistic Personality Traits**

Narcissistic personality traits can feed self-destructive thoughts. Narcissism may seem like too much self-love. But it often comes from deep self-doubt and insecurity. This leads to a fragile self-image that needs ongoing praise.

People with narcissistic traits constantly seek affirmation and attention. Their self-worth depends on others' approval. When approval is lacking, self-destructive thoughts can take over. Feelings of unworthiness, self-hate, and anger follow.

## Chapter 13 Break Self-Destructive Thoughts

When a person feels very self-important and craves constant praise and admiration. Narcissists may believe they are extra special and deserve special treatment. When they don't get the constant validation they want, they feel hurt and lash out.

To change narcissistic patterns, it helps to develop more empathy. Understanding that others have needs too, not just you, is key. Also, find ways to feel good that don't depend on others' opinions. Focus on your own values and take pride in your real accomplishments. Don't just seek praise - do meaningful things.

Build a balanced, inner sense of self-worth. Don't rely on external praise or attention. With self-insight, narcissistic thought cycles are easier to stop. This prevents them from becoming self-destructive actions.

**Avoid Borderline Personality Behaviours**

Another mental framework that can generate and maintain self-harming thoughts is borderline personality disorder (BPD). Although not everyone who has self-destructive thoughts has BPD, grasping the condition provides critical insights into how emotional instability and black-and-white thinking can nourish destructive mental cycles. People with borderline tendencies often go through intense emotional swings and may find it hard to maintain a stable sense of identity. Their thoughts can rapidly oscillate between extremes, like idealization and criticism, making it tough to have a steady and constructive inner conversation.

Learning to manage emotions and thoughts effectively is vital in breaking the chain of self-harming thinking. Using a balanced approach to emotional experiences, rather than jumping to extremes, can significantly decrease the frequency and intensity of self-destructive thoughts. This prevents them from becoming self-destructive actions.

Borderline thinking can be very black-and-white. People are either perfect or terrible, with nothing in between. Moods swing rapidly between idealizing and hating the same person. Fears of abandonment are intense.

To break this cycle, try to see shades of gray. People are complex combinations of good and bad qualities. Moods naturally shift sometimes too. Practice radical acceptance - allowing life's ups and downs without exaggerating their meaning. Stay grounded in the present moment.

**Avoid Attention-Seeking**

Sometimes, people think in ways that are harmful to themselves. These self-destructive thoughts can take different forms. Let's explore some common types of self-destructive thinking and how people can move past them.

Attention-seeking can lead to self-destructive thoughts. When craving attention gets extreme, failure to get it can spiral into very negative thinking. This often links to underlying issues like low self-worth.

Build a solid sense of self-esteem to avoid attention-seeking traps. Identify your values and real skills. Celebrate achievements that don't depend on others' views. Practice self-compassion. Set reasonable goals and work towards them. This lasting self-confidence makes outside attention less necessary.

Many types of unhealthy thinking patterns exist. We need to make positive changes tailored to each issue we struggle with. Develop empathy and self-love. See life's shades of gray. Find internal validation. With self-insight and the right tools, anyone can dismantle attention-seeking thinking habits and build more constructive thought patterns. The result is greater mental health and more power to direct your life in positive ways.

**Our Choices Affect Our Thinking**

Making choices shapes how we think. Each choice we make - or avoid making - sends ripples through our future actions and thoughts. For example, deciding to tackle a tough problem might first make us anxious or scared. But it can eventually lead to feelings of strength and higher self-esteem. On the other hand, dodging challenges or taking the easy way out can reinforce thoughts that we're not good enough or have no power.

## Chapter 13 Break Self-Destructive Thoughts

Making conscious choices takes knowing ourselves. This self-awareness often comes through reflective practices like journaling, meditation, or therapy. It also means weighing how choices will impact us not just right away, but in the long run. Being proactive in making choices that match our goals and values can greatly reduce negative thoughts. It can also nurture a more positive mindset.

While outside situations do shape our options, we have personal responsibility in directing our thinking. Admitting we're accountable for our choices is the first step toward changing future decisions and their effects on our thoughts. Taking responsibility flips us from a passive mindset, which can feed destructive thoughts, to an active one. This active stance is essential for constructive change.

Accountability should not be a platform for self-blame. Rather, it empowers us. It gives us control to shift behaviours and thought patterns. Reframing techniques can help us see poor choices or mistakes as chances to learn and grow. This transforms thoughts of regret into thoughts of opportunity.

Owning our choices requires courage and humility. But the personal growth and self-knowledge gained are invaluable. We can build emotional resilience when we reflect on choices candidly yet compassionately. This process reveals our core values and motivations. It also uncovers unconscious biases we may hold.

With time and practice, we can become more adept at making choices aligned with our best self. The better we know ourselves, the better we can anticipate whether a choice will lead to constructive or destructive thought patterns. We can catch and reshape negative thinking before it takes hold.

No one is perfect. There will always be choices we later wish we could change. Self-judgment only repeats old thought loops. Instead, we can focus on the insights gained for making wiser choices moving forward. We can also extend the same gentle understanding to others making difficult choices.

In this way, conscious choice-making creates a upwards spiral. As we become more mindful of our thought patterns, we can steadily shift our thinking in a positive direction. The more constructively we think, the better choices we tend to make. Our choices then reinforce and reflect our personal growth.

**The Power of Apologies and Forgiveness**

Apologizing and forgiving can have big effects on how we think. Saying "I'm sorry" in a real way can free your mind from feelings of guilt or regret. Forgiving someone can help stop thoughts of anger or wanting to get even. Even when you know you are right, choosing to say sorry can reduce tension, inside yourself and with others. It can open the door to more helpful thoughts.

Similarly, forgiveness does not say the other person was right. But it frees us from carrying around negative feelings. It cleans out our emotions in a way. This makes room for more positive, constructive thinking. Things like empathy training can make it easier to forgive. Forgiving reduces stress and improves mental health a lot.

Saying "I'm sorry" can also be a tool to manage negative thoughts. It can mark the moment we realize our thinking has become negative or self-destructive. It signals it's time to switch to a more constructive way of thinking, by acknowledging the negative thought and committing to changing that thought pattern going forward.

The capacity to apologize and forgive are important emotional skills. Saying "I'm sorry" sincerely can free your mind from guilt. Forgiving cleanses negative emotions to make way for positivity. Apologizing reduces tension and opens the door to constructive thoughts. Forgiving decreases stress and improves well-being.

Apologizing marks negative thoughts, signaling it's time to change thinking. Forgiving declutters emotions to clear space for growth. Together they transform thinking in a multi-step process. It takes self-awareness, responsible choices, and emotional intelligence. When

## Chapter 13 Break Self-Destructive Thoughts

understood deeply, apologizing and forgiving build a framework for dismantling destructive thoughts. This understanding enables nourishing new mental landscapes to emerge.

Saying "I'm sorry" and "I forgive you" are powerful phrases. They can rewrite mental patterns that limit us. Apology liberates, reducing inner turmoil. Forgiveness cleanses, inviting spaces for renewal. Both require courage and vulnerability. Their transformative potential is unlocked through empathy. With compassion, they become tools to recalibrate the mind. Wielded with care, they can cultivate thinking anew.

These small phrases unlock tremendous inner power. Apology liberates us from the past's weight. Forgiveness lifts the heart's heaviness. Together they allow new choices, new space. With courage, we unlock their potential for growth. When we apologize and forgive authentically, we transform. Our minds become free to create, connect, and nourish. We cultivate new landscapes of thought.

# Thoughts and Not Feelings

Thoughts and feelings work together. This matters in our daily lives. It changes how we make choices and get along with others. Since they matter so much, we should understand how they work together. This chapter explains the difference between thoughts and feelings. It looks at overthinking too much. It also compares impulsive and well-thought-out thoughts. By the end, you will better understand your thoughts and feelings. This will help you make wiser choices and feel more balanced.

**What's the Difference Between a Thought and a Feeling?**

The difference between thoughts and feelings may seem small, but understanding this basic difference has a big impact on our mental health. Thoughts are cognitive and can be expressed clearly in words. They may be the result of reasoning and can often be categorized as facts or opinions. For example, "I need to finish this project by tomorrow" is a thought based on a specific situation and a real deadline.

Feelings, on the other hand, are emotional reactions that may not necessarily be grounded in rational thought. They are our internal responses that show up physically and emotionally. For instance, you

## Chapter 14 Thoughts And Not Feelings

might feel stressed about the project mentioned above. That stress is not a thought; it's an emotional state that comes from our thoughts and possibly other factors like past experiences, our natural tendency towards work, and even our current physical state like sleep quality or general health.

Understanding the difference can lead to more effective emotional control. By labeling experiences accurately as thoughts or feelings, we can better manage our reactions to different situations. This difference can guide our coping strategies. If we're dealing with a negative thought, we might counter it with factual evidence. Managing a feeling might involve physical activities like deep breathing or going for a walk.

**Control Overthinking - Reduce Worrying**

Overthinking can take over and cause anxiety and stress. It happens when we dwell too much on decisions, issues, or fears. This gets in the way of handling life and work well. Overthinking can happen in personal or professional situations. It often leads to being unable to act because we may fear all the possible outcomes too much.

There are ways to address overthinking. One effective strategy is mindfulness. This involves focusing on the present moment without judgment. Mindfulness practices like deep breathing, grounding exercises, or meditation can stop the cycle of overthinking. They draw our attention away from the looping thoughts and into the here and now.

Another approach is cognitive restructuring. This cognitive-behavioural technique identifies and challenges the irrational thinking and distortions that fuel overthinking. We can ask ourselves questions to challenge our thoughts, like "Is this based on facts?" or "What's the worst that could happen, and could I handle it?" By addressing overthinking, we gain control of our thoughts and reduce the stress and anxiety that come with them.

Understanding the difference between thoughts and feelings is vital. So is knowing how to manage feelings. These skills help achieve balance and well-being. Whether it's telling apart emotions and thinking or using mindfulness to stop constant worrying, the insights we gain are invaluable life tools.

**Impulsive Thoughts vs. Processed Thoughts (Think Before You Speak)**

Not all thoughts are equal. Some thoughts happen quickly, without thinking them through. These fast, instinctive thoughts can lead to hasty choices or words we later regret. Other thoughts are well thought-out after careful thinking and reflection.

Fast thoughts aren't always bad. They can lead to honest, candid reactions when we need to decide or respond quickly. But they can also lead to mistakes or hurtful comments without thinking first. Well thought-out thoughts let us better understand situations. This makes it more likely our actions or decisions will be good in the long run.

To manage these different thoughts effectively, it's essential to recognize when they happen. In emotional or fast-moving situations, take a brief pause to think. Even a few seconds can change a fast thought into a more thought-out one. This can make our actions and interactions more positive.

**Your Thoughts Don't Have to Be Your Feelings**

Managing our thoughts and feelings is an important skill. Realizing that our thoughts don't have to control our feelings is a big step. Just because we think something does not mean we have to feel a certain way. We can look at our thoughts critically. Then decide if they should impact how we feel.

For example, you might think, "I made a mistake, so I am a failure." This thought could easily make you feel bad about yourself. But if you really look at the thought, making one mistake does not mean you are a failure. Challenging the thought can help you separate it from the feeling. Then you avoid unnecessary negative feelings.

## Chapter 14 Thoughts And Not Feelings

We need to identify thinking patterns that make us feel bad. By recognizing these patterns, we can reframe our thoughts. This helps neutralize or positively impact our feelings.

Being able to separate thoughts from feelings gives you more control over your emotional well-being. It allows you to interact with the world in a more thoughtful way. Recognizing that thoughts can trigger feelings, but don't have to, lets you choose your emotional reactions carefully. This adds sophistication to your emotional intelligence.

For example, say you are giving an important presentation at work. The thought crosses your mind, "What if I mess up and look incompetent?" This could make you feel nervous and afraid. But instead of accepting that thought, you could challenge it. Is one mistake really proof of incompetence? Does the audience want you to fail? The answer is likely no. Reframing the thought helps avoid unnecessary fear.

### Avoid Making Your Feelings Other People's Issues

Managing feelings is an important part of life. Feelings are personal experiences that come from thoughts, beliefs, and situations around us. When feelings are very strong, we might want to share them with others. But sharing feelings with others can sometimes cause problems, especially if the feelings come more from our own thoughts than from the actual situation.

The key is finding the right balance in sharing feelings. We need to think about when, where, and who to share feelings with to keep relationships healthy and manage our own emotions. Emotional intelligence helps with this. It means understanding our own feelings and being aware of others' feelings too. This helps us decide if it's appropriate to share feelings in a certain case.

If the thoughts behind the feelings come from assumptions, over-generalizations, or unrealistic beliefs, the first step is to examine those thoughts ourselves. If needed, we can ask professionals or trusted people to help us understand these thoughts and feelings better. Their input can give valuable perspective to manage thoughts and feelings more effectively.

Sharing feelings is important for connection and emotional health. But some thoughts that lead to feelings may not connect to the reality of a situation. In those cases, it's best to process those emotions internally before expressing them externally. With self-examination and support, we can learn to transform unhelpful thoughts into constructive thinking patterns. This allows us to share our feelings in a way that builds connections without causing tensions.

Managing emotions requires tuning into our inner world and the world around us. It takes self-awareness, empathy, and discernment. When feelings overwhelm us, we need spaces for introspection and trusted companions for wise counsel. As we understand the roots of our emotions, we can nurture the ones that reflect reality and transform the ones that distort it. This allows us to express our authentic feelings skillfully and sensitively attuned to others and the context.

Our emotions give colour to our inner landscape. But not all emotions help us see clearly or act rightly. Self-management allows us to filter our feelings wisely so we can share our hearts without causing harm. With care and discernment, we learn when transparent vulnerability nurtures intimacy, and when discretion protects relationships. Emotional intelligence guides us to relate with truth and grace.

**Don't Live by Feelings**

Feelings can show our inner state and motivate us. But living only by feelings is risky. Feelings change quickly based on outside events and thoughts. Making long-term choices or usual reactions only by feelings can be inconsistent and lead to regret.

Instead, we need to match our actions and choices to our values, goals, and logical thinking. This doesn't mean ignoring feelings. It means seeing feelings as one thing to think about when living life. Doing this makes a

## Chapter 14 Thoughts And Not Feelings

steady framework for acting that is less likely to change with the ups and downs of emotions.

**Feelings as Indicators of Insecurities**

Sometimes feelings that keep coming back can be signs of deeper worries or unsolved problems. When certain feelings keep happening again and again, especially without a clear reason from outside, it's good to look into the thoughts causing these feelings. Are these thoughts based on past experiences, what society expects, or fears without proof? Finding these out can be the first step to solving the worries themselves.

In cases like these, the thoughts and feelings make each other stronger in a loop. Breaking this cycle takes real effort to face the thoughts fueling your worries. Thinking techniques can be very helpful here. They allow you to challenge and reframe the thoughts that bring up the difficult feelings.

Understanding the differences between thoughts and feelings clearly, and knowing how to control feelings, are important steps in achieving emotional balance and wellness. Whether it's telling emotional states and thinking processes apart, or using mindfulness to stop constant worrying, the skills you'll learn from these insights are invaluable life tools.

By recognizing and understanding the differences and connections between thoughts and feelings, we can gain more control over both. This control isn't about ignoring or denying but about managing wisely. Understanding the nature, origins, and impacts of our thoughts lets us live a life guided by thoughtful intention, not ruled by passing emotions.

Chapter 15

# Changing Your Habits and Behaviours

Negative habits and behaviours often get in the way of improving our lives. Not doing things we need to do, eating unhealthy foods, or always being negative are examples. These patterns make it hard to reach our goals and live the life we want. So how do these behaviours start and, more importantly, how can we change them? This chapter looks at how our habits and behaviours work. It examines our thought patterns that lead to habits. It also gives ideas for making real change. Understanding our own actions and thoughts helps us make big shifts in our daily lives.

**What Are Negative Habits and Behaviours?**

Bad habits and behaviours hurt our life, health, relationships, and goals. These behaviours are often ways to cope with bigger problems—emotional, mental, or physical. For example, stress eating is not just about food. It is a way to deal with feeling upset or anxious. Also, putting things off is not just being lazy. It is often a way to avoid fear of failure or feeling

## Chapter 15 Changing Your Habits And Behaviours

not good enough. Understanding this link—how a behaviour helps and hurts—is key to making real change.

These bad behaviours build on each other. For example, poor sleep may lead to doing less, which then may cause stress, leading to more bad habits like unhealthy eating or skipping exercise. This downward spiral shows how connected bad habits and behaviours are. Often, it is hard to address one without looking at its link to others.

**We Become What We Think We Are and What We Do**

The idea that "thoughts become things" matters a lot when we talk about habits and behaviours. The picture we have in our minds of ourselves shapes our actions. If you keep thinking you can't do things or you mess up, your actions will match that view. You won't try as hard or even set yourself up to fail. In this way, a negative self-image causes a loop. Your thoughts lead to actions, and your actions reinforce those thoughts.

Think of someone who believes they are bad at social situations. This belief makes them nervous to be social. That affects how they act, making them awkward or shy. This confirms their belief that they are bad socially. It's a loop that repeats. The only way to break it is to step in at the thought level to change the behaviour. Or better yet, both.

But you can rewrite this mental picture by challenging and changing negative thought patterns. This makes it easier to develop new behaviours. Self-affirmations, meditation, and exercise can help reshape self-perception. This creates better ground for positive behaviour change.

By exploring these mechanisms, we gain power to step in consciously. We can choose to break the chain by shifting our thoughts. This can lead our behaviour to change. The first step is acknowledging our thoughts shape our actions, and recognizing our capacity to modify those core beliefs.

**Regrets Affect Our Thinking from How We Behave and What We Do**

Regret is a very strong feeling that can really change how we think and act. When we regret something, it means we feel bad about a choice we made because it does not match up with what we hoped would happen or what is important to us. This mismatch between what we did and what we wanted can make us think a lot about the past choice we regret.

When we do things that lead to regret, these bad feelings get stored in our memory, creating a link that can either make us avoid or repeat similar choices later on, depending on the situation.

For example, if someone misses out on a promotion at work because they doubted their abilities, that regret might make them avoid taking chances on future opportunities. On the other hand, regret can also push people to make changes. If someone regrets not living a healthy lifestyle after having a health issue, that regret could motivate them to adopt better habits moving forward. The key is to direct regret's emotional energy into positive change instead of letting it turn into guilt or shame that leads to more negative thoughts and actions.

Learning to deal with regret means recognizing the experience, forgiving yourself, and taking concrete steps to avoid similar situations down the road. Tools like keeping a reflective journal, setting goals, and talking to a mental health professional can help transform regret into a driving force for beneficial changes in behaviour.

When we look back with regret on a choice, it is because we feel remorse over an action that did not align with our values or expectations. This emotional discord compels us to dwell on the past decision. Regretful behaviours become ingrained in our memory, priming us to either avoid or repeat those choices depending on the context.

For instance, regret over missed professional opportunities due to self-doubt may lead to dodging future chances. Conversely, regret about poor health habits after a medical scare could prompt positive lifestyle changes. The key is channeling regret's emotional energy into constructive change rather than unproductive guilt.

Managing regret involves acknowledging the emotion, practicing self-forgiveness, and taking proactive steps to avert recurrences. Tools like reflective journaling, goal-setting, and counseling can help transform regret from a negative force into motivation for behavioural improvements. With self-reflection and a growth mindset, regret can serve as an invaluable teacher rather than a source of anguish.

**Being Kind Will Change Your Mindset**

Practicing kindness, both to yourself and others, can greatly improve your mindset and behaviour. Being kind counteracts negative feelings like anger, resentment, and hostility, which can make you act in harmful ways. Making small, kind acts part of your daily routine can shift your focus away from self-centered or negative thinking, making space for more positive thoughts and actions.

The acts of kindness release endorphins, our body's natural mood boosters, and lower stress hormone levels. This creates an environment in our minds that makes positive thinking and behaviour more likely. When we experience the benefits of kindness, it reinforces the action, making us more likely to repeat it. Over time, this can become a positive cycle that not only helps us but also positively impacts those around us.

Furthermore, being kind builds empathy and understanding, improving your relationships. Better relationships can lead to a more supportive environment, reducing the stress and negativity that often trigger undesirable habits and behaviours. In short, being kind is not just an ethical choice - it's a strategic one for anyone aiming to improve their mindset and behaviours.

The importance of kindness goes beyond mere etiquette and plays a key role in shaping our mindset. By embracing kindness as a core value, we equip ourselves with a powerful tool for fighting negative thoughts and behaviours, enriching not just our lives but also the lives of those around us.

**A Heart of Gratitude Will Help See the Light at the End of the Tunnel**

Focusing on what we are thankful for can improve our mental health. It takes our attention away from what stresses us out. This gives our minds a break from negative thoughts. Being grateful also activates brain chemicals that control our mood and happiness.

Keeping a gratitude journal or making lists of things we are grateful for, trains our brain to focus on the good things in life. By practicing gratitude regularly, we make our brains better at finding positives, even during tough times. Gratitude gives us a hopeful mindset to deal with life's challenges. It helps us see solutions when negativity blinds us. Feeling grateful makes our minds resilient to handle whatever comes our way.

**Change Negative Behaviours**

Changing our habits and behaviours can be really tough. We all have things we'd like to do less of or quit altogether. And we all have positive habits we want to build. This might be procrastinating less, stopping unhealthy relationships, or building better self-care routines.

These kinds of changes don't happen overnight. They take work, self-awareness, and the right strategies.

First, think about the behaviour you want to change. Is it checking social media too much? Arguing with your partner? Skipping your workout? Not speaking up at work?

Then, try to understand why you do this. What triggers the behaviour? How are you feeling right before it happens? There are usually deeper reasons and emotions driving our actions.

For example, scrolling social media when you're bored or avoiding other tasks. You might argue with your partner when you're stressed. You may skip workouts when you're low on energy. Identifying the origins of behaviours is an important first step.

Next, build self-awareness around the behaviour. When does it happen? How often? What precedes it? What do you get out of it? How does it impact your life? Noticing patterns helps you change them.

## Chapter 15 Changing Your Habits And Behaviours

You can also think about the short and long-term consequences of the behaviour. Does checking social media make you feel better temporarily but worse overall? How does procrastination affect your goals? Being aware of the results can help motivate change.

Then, make a plan to alter the habit. If you get the urge to do something negative, pause and make a conscious choice. Over time, these small choices compound to form a new habit.

You could also replace a negative behaviour with a positive one. Feeling lonely? Call a friend instead of eating junk food. Stressed? Go for a walk rather than snapping at your partner. Substituting positive actions rewires your habits.

Consider involving others for support and accountability. Share your goals, ask for encouragement, or join a group. Having people on your side makes change easier.

It also helps to celebrate small wins. Notice when you do something positive, even if it's just for a day. Give yourself credit for little steps forward. Progress takes time, but it's completely within your power to achieve.

Changing behaviours requires self-motivation, patience, and an understanding of our inner drives. But it's possible to replace negative patterns with positive new habits. And it's so worth it.

**Break Bad Habits**

Changing our habits and behaviours can be tough, but it's an important part of personal growth. Bad habits act like shortcuts in our brains - they give us quick relief or satisfaction, but hurt us in the long run. These habits can range from small annoyances to dangerous behaviours. But they all work the same way: something triggers the habit, we do our habitual routine, and then we get a reward that reinforces the habit loop in our brains.

To change a habit, we first need to understand its parts. What causes the habit to happen? What do we actually do in the habit? What do we get out of it? Once we know the trigger, routine, and reward, we can start to change things. The next step is to substitute a new, healthy routine that gives us a similar reward. Sticking to the new routine consistently is key to retraining our brains. Support from friends, family, or professionals also really helps in staying accountable.

Breaking a bad habit takes work, but it teaches us a lot about ourselves too. By figuring out the root causes and making a commitment to change, we can break the habit cycle and develop more positive thinking.

Tackling unhealthy behaviours and bad habits through self-reflection, substitute routines, social support, and sheer determination can improve our lives tremendously. It requires changing our thought patterns at a fundamental level. With time and effort, we can transform our habits and behaviours for the better. This contributes to a more fulfilling, meaningful existence.

In conclusion, changing habits and behaviours is challenging but worthwhile. First it takes self-awareness - understanding our own triggers, routines, and motivations. Then concrete action based on that insight. Shifting attitudes to be more kind and grateful helps too, giving us drive and emotional strength. Breaking habits isn't just about willpower; it means reshaping thoughts, feelings, and actions in new ways. It's hard work but brings big rewards in wellbeing and life satisfaction.

## Chapter 15 Changing Your Habits And Behaviours

Chapter 16

# Be Your Own Hero

Heroes are people who do good things, even when it is hard. They are brave and honest and care about helping others instead of themselves. Big heroes in stories fight monsters and save people. But everyday heroes also do small acts of kindness and courage.

All heroes have strengths and weaknesses, just like everyone else. Looking at these helps us understand what makes someone a hero. It shows that being a hero is complicated. Their good and bad qualities together drive them to do heroic things. Understanding this gives us a deeper view of heroes. It is more than just saying if they are "good" or "bad".

**How to Become a Hero in My Thinking**

To become a hero in your thinking, first understand your current thoughts and beliefs. Observe and journal about yourself or get a psychological assessment. Knowing where you are now is key to setting goals and tracking progress.

## Chapter 16 Be Your Own Hero

Like any hero, have clear goals. Do you want to be more resilient, reduce anxiety, or improve problem-solving? Well-defined goals help us focus mental energy where needed. They also let us measure growth.

Heroes have virtues like courage, wisdom, resilience. Identify virtues that fit your heroism. Actively develop them through exercises, meditation, and real-world challenges.

Mental fitness takes regular training, just like physical fitness. Establish daily practices that build your desired habits. Try mindfulness, reasoning tasks, affirmations that instill courage and self-worth.

Don't avoid challenges. Embrace them as chances to practice, learn, and grow. Apply your new skills and virtues to meet challenges effectively.

Regularly assess progress toward your goals. This maintains focus and allows adaptations. If something isn't working, be willing to change it or try something new. Adaptability is heroic.

Heroes rarely go into it alone, they seek guidance from trusted mentors and engage with like-minded people to get new perspectives and support.

Once mastered, share your insights and strategies. True heroism means uplifting others. Become a guide to extend your heroism beyond your mind.

Becoming a thinking hero is a continuous process of growth and improvement. It takes calculated, committed work to reshape your thinking. By systematically developing heroic virtues and skills, you can face life's challenges with grace, resilience and wisdom.

### Strengths of a Hero

Courage allows heroes to face challenges directly. They can deal with physical danger, difficult choices, or emotional struggles. Courage helps heroes put others' wellbeing before their own needs when making hard decisions. Integrity means heroes stick to ethical and moral principles. This makes them a moral guide in their communities. Resilience helps heroes bounce back from setbacks and keep working toward their goals. It keeps them motivated. Empathy and compassion give heroes emotional intelligence. This allows them understand and care about others' needs and feelings. It drives them to make sacrifices for the greater good. Heroes often have strong leadership skills. This lets them rally and guide others toward good outcomes through clear communication and strategic thinking.

**Weaknesses of a Hero**

While being brave is good, it can sometimes become reckless. Not judging risks well can lead to unnecessary danger or loss, hurting not just the heroes but also those they want to protect. The tendency to sacrifice yourself too much can also be a weakness when done extremely, possibly leading to physical or emotional exhaustion and reducing the hero's long-term effectiveness.

Idealism is another double-edged sword. While a strong moral guide is valuable, extreme idealism can cloud judgment and limit the hero's ability to seek practical solutions that require a nuanced ethical approach. A hero's high personal standards can lead to perfectionism, resulting in self-doubt or too much self-criticism when they think they have fallen short, which can impact their mental well-being.

Narrow focus can also be a potential drawback. An intense focus on a specific cause or mission might limit a hero's perspective, causing them to overlook other important aspects or neglect other life areas.

In short, the qualities that often make someone heroic can, under certain circumstances, also be their weaknesses. This nuanced understanding of strengths and weaknesses not only enriches our idea of what it means to be a hero but also provides a plan for personal growth and self-awareness. The lesson here is the need for balance and recognizing that the attributes contributing to heroism require careful management and mindfulness.

**Strengths and Weaknesses of My Thoughts**

## Chapter 16 Be Your Own Hero

Analyzing how our thoughts help or limit us can teach a lot about how we think and feel. This can help us improve ourselves in meaningful ways. If we are good at figuring out complicated problems, we can use logic to handle challenges and find solutions. Being able to understand how others feel can help us build strong relationships and work well on teams.

Positive thinking can make us more resilient, allowing us to manage stress better and be more satisfied with life. An open mind eager to explore new ideas, learn, and consider different views creates opportunities for growth. Self-reflection helps us critically examine our actions and choices to learn from our mistakes and successes.

However, some thought patterns can hold us back from growing personally and intellectually. Overthinking, while a sign of an analytical mind, can also lead to excessive rumination that prevents action and decisions. Focusing on the negatives can increase stress, anxiety, and lost chances for happiness and fulfillment. An inability to adapt our thinking when faced with new information can limit personal growth. If our thoughts are heavily swayed by our emotions, we may struggle to respond rationally to stressful situations, hurting our relationships and wellbeing. A tendency to seek out or interpret information to confirm existing beliefs can lead to a narrow perspective and resistance to change or growth.

Understanding these aspects of our thinking provides a comprehensive view of how our thought processes impact our actions and emotions. The goal is not just to recognize our strengths but to pinpoint areas for improvement and develop strategies to address them.

Identifying our thought patterns' strengths allows us to build on them through deliberate practice and application. For example, if we are skilled at problem-solving, consciously putting ourselves in situations that test those skills could lead to professional success or personal satisfaction. On the other hand, knowing our cognitive weaknesses allows us to take corrective steps. If we tend to overthink, mindfulness exercises could provide substantial benefits. If negativity is a challenge, reframing our thoughts can train us to focus on a more balanced, constructive outlook.

Evaluating the pros and cons of our thoughts offers a valuable roadmap for cognitive and emotional development. It provides the self-awareness to enhance your wellbeing, relationships, and potential.

**Turn Obstacles Into Opportunities**

Turning problems into possibilities is one of the key traits of a hero. When you come across a tough situation, don't see it as a wall blocking your way. Look at it as a test of what you can do, a chance to get stronger or learn new skills. Having this attitude doesn't just help you conquer the issue today; it also gives you strong mental tools to take on future challenges. This is more than just being optimistic. It's changing how you think about solving issues in a way that turns roadblocks into launch pads for growth.

By being your own hero means taking charge of your mental approach. It's focusing on moving forward and taking positive action instead of dwelling on setbacks or limits. By tapping into your cognitive strengths and diligently improving your mental weaknesses, you set the stage for heroic deeds in all parts of life. You learn to transform trials into opportunities to grow and better yourself. This leads to you playing a heroic role in your own life story. It takes ongoing effort and self-reflection, but the internal and external rewards make it very worthwhile.

We can start by taking an inventory of our current thought processes. Which mental strategies are serving you well? Which thought habits are holding you back from your goals? Make a list of both to clearly see what's working and what needs improvement. For example, you may have a tendency to ruminate on past mistakes, which sinks your motivation, or you default to doubting your abilities when challenges arise. These would be prime weaknesses to target.

On the flip side, you have a knack for creatively brainstorming solutions, or you're good at compartmentalizing worries so they don't distract you from the task at hand. Lean into these cognitive strengths whenever you can. Let them form the foundation as you work to improve your weaker thought patterns.

## Chapter 16 Be Your Own Hero

When looking to enhance our mental skills, we need to make goals that are specific, measurable, and time bound. Rather than vague resolutions like "think more positively," we need to give ourselves concrete steps. For instance, "Next time I start mentally criticizing myself, I'll replace each negative thought with two positive counter-statements." Track your progress in a journal to stay accountable. Celebrate each small win.

As your thought habits improve, put them into practice when obstacles arise. For example, you have a big presentation next week and you're feeling overwhelmed. Instead of dwelling on how unprepared you feel, reframe it as a challenge to grow your public speaking skills. Make a timeline of steps you can take before the presentation to get ready. Focus on what you can control. Each time nerves creep in, take a deep breath and remind yourself of times you've overcome anxiety in the past.

This sort of obstacle is a perfect opportunity to flex your upgraded mental muscles. Lean into your go-to cognitive strengths like compartmentalizing worries or brainstorming ideas. At the same time, implement coping thoughts to short-circuit unhelpful rumination. Use the situation to practice redirecting your mindset. When the day arrives, you'll feel empowered to succeed.

With consistent effort, these new thought habits will become second nature. You'll instinctively know how to transform obstacles into opportunities for achievement. Friends and family may start calling you their personal hero because you always have creative solutions and unstoppable determination. Most importantly, you'll feel immense pride from taking charge of your mental game.

Remember, it's normal to backslide occasionally. Change takes time. If old negative thought patterns creep back in, don't beat yourself up. Be patient and simply refocus on your goals. Track what situations tend to trigger unhelpful thinking so you can catch it quickly next time. You may stumble but staying committed to growth means you'll always get back up stronger than before.

To conclude, being a hero in our own lives are about living more consciously. We need to make our thought patterns and mental habits an object of daily focus. We need to aim to understand ourselves on a deeper level so we can optimize the way our minds work. We need to know both our cognitive superpowers and kryptonite weaknesses. With this self-knowledge, we can tap into our strengths and develop strategies to counteract our vulnerabilities. Leaning into this active mental approach paves the way for heroic thinking and action.

The path of continuous growth and self-improvement is not always smooth. But by sticking to it, we'll reach new heights of achievement and fulfillment. With the mindset of a hero, no obstacle can block our way for long. Each challenge simply helps forge us into a stronger version of ourselves. So be your own hero and meet life's difficulties head-on, knowing you have the mental tools and fortitude to transform trials into triumphs.

# Chapter 16 Be Your Own Hero

## Chapter 17

# Be Optimistic - Excel in Positive Thinking

The world has many challenges. Everyone faces some kind of adversity. A positive mindset matters a lot in this situation. Optimism is not just for "lucky" people. It is necessary. It is a choice that can change our lives. Understanding optimism and its benefits helps us see it as important for personal growth and social impact. This chapter explains optimism. It looks at where self-worth fits in. It explores how the brain works with optimism. It describes the real rewards optimism brings to life.

**Understand Self-Worth and Self-Value**

Knowing our own self-worth is an important first step to feeling hopeful. When we value ourselves, it helps us in many ways. It allows us to build healthier relationships, make better choices, and live a happier life overall. Valuing ourselves sets the tone for how others should value us too. With self-worth, we aim for goals that truly matter instead of settling for less. Our choices show our belief in ourselves, which keeps this positive cycle going.

# Chapter 17 Be Optimistic - Excel In Positive Thinking

But knowing our self-worth is not always easy. Many people struggle with low self-esteem from bad past experiences, social pressures, or lack of support. In these cases, self-reflection and professional help can unravel the complicated feelings. Learning to separate outside validation from inner worth is key. The first change depending on others, but the second relies on our own inner voice.

## What's the Neurological Basis for Having a Positive Mind and Being Optimistic?

Positive thoughts can actually rewire our brain. They strengthen neural networks that promote mental resilience and wellbeing.

One example is neurotransmitters like dopamine and serotonin. The brain makes these when you have optimistic thoughts. These chemicals are key for regulating mood. And for overall mental health.

Also, parts of the brain like the prefrontal cortex play a big role. This area is linked to higher functions. Like problem-solving, planning, and decision-making. These are essential skills for tackling life's challenges. When made optimistic, the prefrontal cortex improves thinking skills and mental agility. Optimism is not just an emotion; it is a thinking strategy. It uses specific brain mechanisms for our benefit.

By understanding the brain basis of optimism adds incentive to practice positive thinking. Knowing our brains can benefit from optimism may empower people. It can help them break negative thought cycles. Even if it takes effort at first.

By embracing self-worth and the brain basis of optimism. We set the stage for an enriching life from better mental and physical health, to improved relationships and professional success. The benefits of optimism are far-reaching and profound. This chapter explains optimism and invites you to unlock its benefits by cultivating an optimistic mindset.

## The Results and Rewards of Being Positive and Optimistic

The positive effects of being optimistic are real, not just hopeful thinking. Looking on the bright side improves our mental health, relationships, work, and even physical health.

When we are optimistic, we deal with less stress better. Less stress means lower levels of cortisol and balanced hormones, which help our immune system work properly. We can bounce back faster when life gets hard. When we believe things will not work out, we look for solutions instead of giving up. This resilience protects us when challenges come up, as they always do.

Good emotional health is another benefit. When we are optimistic, we are less likely to struggle with depression or anxiety. A positive outlook acts like medicine against these mood problems, helping us feel satisfied and happy overall.

Relationships improve when we're optimistic too. It draws people in, like a magnet. Optimistic people often become leaders, inspiring others with hopeful visions of the future. Their sunny outlook lifts up those around them, improving morale and even productivity.

At work, optimists tend to do better and earn more money. They solve problems creatively, take calculated risks, and seize opportunities. A fearless, "glass half full" attitude leads to success. In finances, optimism helps people make sound money decisions and avoid feeling overwhelmed.

When we are optimistic, we live longer, healthier lives. Each of these interconnected benefits builds on the others, creating an upward spiral towards a rewarding, fulfilling life.

Most importantly, optimism improves our daily experience. With mental toughness, we can handle stress better and recover faster from problems. We see challenges as temporary setbacks rather than crushing defeats, making life's journey more enjoyable, even fun.

## Chapter 17 Be Optimistic - Excel In Positive Thinking

To conclude, looking on the bright side enriches life in many ways. It affects our health, friends, career, and more. Our brains reward positive thinking, both emotionally and physically.

Though the world often feels full of challenges, recognizing our self-worth and embracing optimism gives us the power to succeed. A positive mindset is not just nice, but a strategy to actively improve our whole life.

So adopt an attitude of hope. Expect good things and look for solutions when trouble strikes. With optimism, we can navigate life's journey successfully and enjoy ourselves along the way.

## Chapter 18

# See Yourself How Others See You

Self-improvement is a cycle of thinking about yourself, growing, and changing. This chapter, "See Yourself How Others See You," has tools to help you look at yourself in a meaningful way and make positive changes. The chapter is a guide to help us grow as a person. It starts with an honest self-assessment to help us understand our strengths and weaknesses. This will allow us to make plans to improve ourselves. By following these steps, we can become a better person and have a positive impact on the people around us. Let's take a closer look at the first two parts of this chapter: self-assessment and the steps to making lasting changes.

**Do a Self-Assessment and Admit Your Flaws, Weaknesses, Mistakes, Bad Habits, and Incompetence**

To grow, the first step is for us to assess ourselves honestly. Don't just glance in the mirror; take a deep dive into your actions, skills, and mindset. We can use the structured methods like SWOT analysis (Strengths, Weaknesses, Opportunities, and Threats.) Strengths and weaknesses are within our control and can be changed. Opportunities and threats are outside factors we must adapt to. Using such a framework makes the process easier and more organized. Admitting our flaws is not a sign of weakness; it's the first step to self-improvement. Without this admission, we risk becoming stagnant and failing to grow personally and professionally.

**Work on Changing Yourself to Become Better**

After finding our weak points, the next logical step is to start a systematic plan to get better. However, change does not happen overnight or alone. It needs time, effort, and often, help from others. In our careers, this could mean getting more training or education to fill in skill gaps. Or it could mean working with a mentor who can give us tailored advice and direction.

In our personal life, change may need a reset of our relationships or hard work on emotional intelligence. The key is making SMART goals (Specific, Measurable, Achievable, Relevant, and Time-Bound.) These goals should target the weaknesses we found. They will map out change. Regular progress checks, either self-done or with mentors, can help us stay on track. We can adjust the plan as needed.

By accepting self-assessment and committing to change, we make a solid framework for personal growth. This process not only improves our lives, but it also sets a positive example for those around us. It creates a ripple effect of improvement that can go far beyond ourselves.

After finding weaknesses, logically start a plan to improve. Change takes time, effort, and often outside help.

**Explore the Seeds of Greatness in You**

Each person has special talents, qualities, and abilities that make them unique. Unfortunately, many people do not develop these natural gifts. They may not know about their talents, or they may face limits like lack of opportunities or resources that hold them back. Finding your innate skills takes self-reflection and trying new things. Personality tests, talent assessments, and hands-on learning can help uncover our natural abilities.

Once we know our talents, the next step is developing them. This often means moving outside our comfort zone. We may need to take on challenges that seem hard at first. For example, if public speaking comes naturally to you, you might have to face your fear of the stage to get better at it. Or if you have a talent in a subject or technical field, you may need special training to sharpen your skills. Mentors and coaches who are experts can also guide us which helps avoid common mistakes and improve faster. By steadily investing time and effort, we can turn our raw talents into strengths. This will drive our personal and professional life to succeed.

Nurturing our abilities requires action. It means seeking opportunities to practice and improve our abilities to do things and be proactive. We can join a club or community related to our interests. We can find competitions and events to showcase our skills. We can seek out classes and training programs to expand our knowledge. We can read books by experts in the field we have an interest in. We can watch talented people to learn from them, their successes and failures which can provide useful lessons.

Set goals to motivate our development break major goals into smaller milestones and track our progress. We need to celebrate each achievement along the way and stay focused on improving a little at a time. We need t avoid comparing ourselves to others. Everyone learns at their own pace. We need to be patient with ourselves when we hit plateaus. We should reflect on what works so we can keep improving.

We need to surround ourselves with supportive people and share our aspirations with family and friends. Let them cheer us on as we work toward our potential. Their belief in you can boost your confidence and resilience.

We need to collaborate with peers who have similar interests. We can learn from each other. We should connect with mentors who have

Chapter 18 See Yourself How Others See You

experience to offer. They can provide insider tips and feedback to accelerate our growth.

We should be maximizing our abilities by making commitments. We can expect setbacks and challenges as we push our limits. We need to be persistent through frustrations and adversity and draw strength from our passion where it drives us to keep reaching higher.

We need to stay open and keep learning as we gain skills, and new interests emerge. We should be nurturing all facets of our talents and keep fine-tuning and expanding our abilities, no matter how adept we become. We have gifts only we can offer the world. Fulfilling our potential is a lifelong journey of discovery.

**Leave a Good Taste in Others**

Focusing our efforts is key to improving ourselves in all areas of life. This includes bettering our talents, career, relationships, emotions, and health. Setting goals and concentrating on them is crucial as it helps us maximize our potential at home, work, and play.

We need to be careful not to get tunnel vision. While passion for one part of life is great, neglecting others causes problems. It can throw off balance and limit our growth. The ideal approach is setting varied goals across all facets. For example, if you aim for a promotion, also plan family time, self-care, and fun. Use tools to help, like schedules, lists, and reflection periods. This balanced view makes the most of our energies.

The right goals enhance the whole you. This goes beyond just separate skills. The aim is a rich life, not isolated gains. With focus spread evenly, we evolve completely. Every area improves together through a steady march forward.

Starting out, assess where you need growth. Make notes on skills, career, health, knowledge, relationships, and interests. What strengths need polish? Which parts need more attention? What new horizons do you want to explore? Perhaps take training classes, get certified in new software, take on key projects, and schedule special events.

# I Am Not My Thoughts

Also set emotional and self-care goals. Do you want to manage stress better, make new friends, take a daily walk, or journal? Whatever it is, articulate an exact plan. Break big goals into steps. Track progress through metrics like completion dates, times, or amounts.

With SMART goals for each area, schedule time to work on them. Balance is crucial, so we need to divide effort appropriately. Don't let one goal dominate time and energy. Use calendars, daily plans, and reminders to stay on track. Schedule rewards when you achieve milestones.

As you pursue goals, check in with yourself often. Are you keeping balance across all facets? Does tunnel vision set in at times? Adjust each psychosocial goals constantly to maintain an even hand. Completing steps in one area should never sideline progress in others.

Reflect regularly on the big picture, too. Do your goals still align with who you want to become? Do growth areas need reassessment? Be ready to refresh goals when life changes. Keep the end vision in sight: a fulfilling life where no area lacks.

With consistent effort across all realms, your potential unfolds. Each small gain builds on the last. Bit by bit, you sculpt the ideal life. It takes patience and perseverance, but you will evolve fully, and with balance, no part of you gets left behind.

We need to stay confident when progress seems slow and remember that each small steps add up. Even if one area lags, keep nurturing it while excelling elsewhere. Everything contributes to growth and self-discovery.

Soon your improved skills will make work more rewarding, creating healthy habits that will boost our energy and mood. Our emotional intelligence will increase, bringing deeper connections as new horizons expand our worldview.

By lifting up each area of life, we elevate our whole existence. The journey brings insight into who we are and what matters most. Our potential will blossom fully across the board. We need to remember a consistent balanced effort is the key. We should keep focus wide, stay

## Chapter 18 See Yourself How Others See You

determined, and enjoy the fruits of our labour. The effort will sculpt a rich and fulfilling life.

**Help Others to Become Better Than Yourself**

Personal growth is often seen as an individual journey. But there is great value in joining together on the path of self-improvement. By becoming a mentor, we can actively help others on their own journey. Mentoring provides a special chance to watch someone's life positively change through our guidance and encouragement.

We should carry an attitude of making others better than ourselves, helping them to see more than we have seen and to accomplish more than we have accomplished.

As a mentor, we don't just give advice, we help others understand their talents and potential. We help them work through problems and make plans for the future. Mentoring is one of the most rewarding parts of personal development. It allows us to directly take part in someone's growth.

But the goal is not just to assist others reach their current goals, but to help them go beyond what we have achieved. This is more than teaching; it builds a legacy. When we help others succeed in ways we couldn't, it creates a lasting impact.

Maybe you faced limits on resources, opportunities, or time. By guiding others past those limits, our influence is multiplied. This creates a ripple effect of positive change that can reach far beyond what we could do alone. The people we mentor may go on to open doors for many more. Our support starts a chain reaction of improvement across many lives.

Mentoring others on their personal growth journey creates a legacy. Your knowledge and encouragement help our mentees surpass our own achievements. This multiplies our positive impact as they pass on what they've learned. Working together, step by step, creates powerful progress.

**Live by the Golden Rule**

The saying "Treat others the way you want to be treated" contains great wisdom and may seem simple. But its effects are far-reaching and can deeply change both people and communities for the better. This idea serves as an ethical foundation that goes across cultures, religions, and philosophies. In a world increasingly divided by different viewpoints and beliefs, the Golden Rule provides a universal guide for ethics that promotes harmony and mutual respect.

In everyday interactions, following this rule lays the groundwork for healthy relationships. Whether with family, friends, or coworkers, mutual respect and understanding naturally happen when everyone follows this idea. Simple acts, like listening closely when someone else speaks or showing kindness to a stranger, can start a chain reaction of positivity. As we match our actions to this rule, we gain a reputation for fairness and empathy. This can positively impact our social and professional life.

Moreover, the Golden Rule is not just about reactive reciprocity - treating others well in hopes they will do the same for us. It is proactive. It encourages us to take the first step, to initiate kindness and respect in all interactions, regardless of others' behaviour or attitudes. This proactivity presents a subtle yet strong form of social leadership, setting a standard for others to follow, even without formal authority.

When applied in a professional setting, the Golden Rule improves our corporate culture and teamwork. It replaces competition with collaboration, thereby emphasizing collective achievements over our triumphs. Employees working in an environment of respect and dignity are more likely to be engaged and productive. This in turn increases an organization's overall efficiency and effectiveness.

Adopting this principle as a way of life also builds our emotional intelligence. Putting ourselves in another's position exercises empathy, self-awareness, and situational judgment. This enhanced emotional intelligence increases our ability to manage complicated social situations, resolve conflicts, and constructively contribute to our communities.

## Chapter 18 See Yourself How Others See You

Emotional intelligence is not just a personal trait but a social skill to build more meaningful and harmonious relationships.

Living by the Golden Rule does not mean compromising self-interest or becoming overly submissive. It means aligning our self-interest in a way that benefits others too. It does not encourage blind sacrifice but advocates for ethical win-win scenarios where mutual benefit is the goal. Therefore, living by the Golden Rule is also a sophisticated strategy for long-term personal and social well-being.

Personal growth has wide-ranging benefits when we think about it in terms of helping others and making the world a better place. If we expand our ability to empathize to include all people, animals, and the environment, it becomes a powerful tool for bringing people together and promoting peace.

Giving to others often provides rewards, both concrete and abstract. However, giving becomes even more meaningful when done without expecting anything in return. This type of selfless generosity can be profoundly freeing. It changes giving from a transaction to an inherent pursuit, making the act of giving itself the prize.

When we do kind acts or give to others with no strings attached, it changes not just the receiver's life but also our own emotional landscape. We gain a sense of contentment and joy that does not rely on external validation or reciprocal actions. This mindset does not rule out the possibility of positive returns; in fact, it increases it. When we give freely, people are more likely to respond with authentic gratitude and respect, which can materialize in various forms over time, even if we never aimed for those outcomes. Essentially, giving without expectation fosters genuine goodwill and enriches our lives by enhancing our relationships and instilling our actions with a deeper sense of purpose.

Treating everyone we meet with dignity and respect is not just ethical; it also benefits our mental well-being. Discrimination, bias, or unfair treatment diminish both the victim and perpetrator, while respect enhances the dignity of both.

Investing in the improvement of others is not just kind; it is also a long-term investment in a better community and, ultimately, a better self. Each act of genuine help contributes to a culture of kindness, respect, and mutual assistance, creating a more harmonious environment for all involved.

The process of our self-improvement not only helps us become a better version of ourselves but also has the potential to positively affect those around us. By adhering to principles of fairness, generosity, and respect, we help make the world a little better, just as that improved world can then contribute to our personal growth.

To conclude, this chapter emphasizes a pivotal approach to our personal growth and social interaction. It stresses the importance of honest self-reflection, continuous self-improvement, and developing innate talents. The chapter underscores that our personal advancement does not occur in isolation. It significantly influences how we interact with others and, as a result, how they see and react to us.

By adopting the principles of self-awareness, focused improvement, generosity, and the Golden Rule, we enhance our own lives while also positively contributing to the lives of those around us. This chapter serves as a reminder that the journey to better our best selves involves not just introspection, but also understanding our influence on others and how their perceptions can provide valuable insights for our development.

Chapter 18 See Yourself How Others See You

# Conclusion

Exploring thoughts and beliefs and how they affect us leads to a better understanding of the complex ways our minds work. Our thought patterns are not random. Many things shape and impact them, from how our brains work to social influences and personal experiences. Seeing how internal and external things—like cognitive biases, personality traits, or other impacts—affect us provides tools to work on mental and emotional growth throughout our lives actively.

Understanding left-brain and right-brain thinking shows us people think in diverse ways. This urges us to value and use our unique sets of strengths and weaknesses. We also gain insight into how deep beliefs, not wanting change, and even generational contexts can solidify our thought patterns, often limiting our potential.

Exploring mental constructs like intrusive thoughts, negative and positive thinking, and self-destructive tendencies illuminates the darker aspects of the human mind. It offers ways to transform and heal. Realizing "I am not my thoughts" is key. It allows distance between the self and thoughts' transient nature, whether stress-related or not. This can aid mental health.

## Conclusion

The idea of being your own hero and championing your thoughts prompts proactive thought and action. It helps us overcome obstacles, making us directors of our destinies. Similarly, seeing the difference between thoughts and feelings enables nuanced emotional intelligence. This allows more balanced, fulfilled lives.

Changing habits and behaviours, embracing optimism, and seeing ourselves as others do are not just personal growth strategies, but are transformative, fundamentally altering how we engage with the world. Understanding their value and using them cultivates a better self, which in turn contributes to a better us.

Therefore, exploring thoughts, beliefs, and influences is an invaluable guide to understanding the intricacies of the human mind. It shows the profound power each of us has, to change, adapt, and grow from wherever we start. As we each take responsibility for our thoughts, integrate positive influences, break free of destructive patterns, and strive to improve ourselves and others, we collectively lay the groundwork for richer understanding, deeper connections, and fulfilling accomplishments.

www.ingramcontent.com/pod-product-compliance
Lightning Source LLC
Chambersburg PA
CBHW011613290426
44110CB00020BA/2580